THE FLATTERING WORD

AND

OTHER ONE-ACT PLAYS

By George Kelly

THE SHOW-OFF — A PLAY

THE FLATTERING WORD AND
other ONE-ACT PLAYS

CRAIG'S WIFE — A DRAMA

DAISY MAYME — A COMEDY

THE FLATTERING WORD

AND

OTHER ONE-ACT PLAYS

BY

GEORGE *Edward* KELLY

BOSTON
LITTLE, BROWN, AND COMPANY
1927

CONTENTS

THE FLATTERING WORD

A SATIRE IN ONE ACT

" . . . that is the flattering word; the one compliment that has never failed.   Tell any man, woman or child that he should be on the stage, — and you'll find him quite as susceptible as a cat is to catnip."

(TESH)

The form of the present manuscript is exactly that in which this satire was presented for two seasons in the principal Keith and Orpheum theaters of The United States of America and The Dominion of Canada.

GEORGE KELLY

TO BOB

"The Flattering Word" was originally presented in New York City.

ORIGINAL CAST

THE REVEREND LORING RIGLEY,
  Pastor of the East Hillcrest Grace
  Reformed Church of Youngs-
  town, Ohio . . . . G. Davison Clarke
MARY, his wife . . . . Doris Dagmar
MRS. ZOOKER, a church-worker . Alice Parks
LENA, her daughter . . . . . . Polly Redfern
EUGENE TESH, a prominent dra-
  matic star . . . . George Kelly

SCENE

A room in the parsonage, on an afternoon in February, — about five o'clock.

THE FLATTERING WORD

When the curtain is well up, Mrs. Rigley, the minister's wife, a very nice, refined-looking woman of probably thirty, dressed in a one-piece dress of navy blue silk, relieved with collar and cuffs of white silk, and wearing her hair very plainly, hurries in through the door at the left and comes forward to the window, where, drawing aside the portière with which the window is hung, she looks out anxiously. At this point, there is a sudden burst of laughter out at the right, which causes her to turn and hurry across to the archway leading to the hall.

RIGLEY (*out at the front door*)

Well, you know, "He who loves the danger shall perish in it!" (*This quotation causes another outburst from the two ladies at the front door*) If you'll excuse me — [*Mrs. Rigley glances out into the hallway; then, taking a folded telegram from the bosom of her dress, she steps back towards the center of the room and commences to read it rather excitedly.*

MRS. ZOOKER (*out at the front door*)

We know what you went through last November!

THE OTHER WOMAN (*at the front door, and speaking simultaneously*)

Don't mention it, Doctor! Not at all, I'm sure.

RIGLEY

It's too much for me!

MRS. ZOOKER

I'll be right in, Reverend.

RIGLEY

You'd better, Mrs. Zooker! you know, "The good die young"!

[*The ladies are again convulsed by the Doctor's brilliancy.*

MRS. ZOOKER

Oh, ain't he terrible!

[*The outer door is heard to close; and, immediately, Mr. Rigley comes laughing into the hallway and hangs his hat upon the hall-tree.*

MARY (*advancing and taking the rather large, flat black book which he extends to her*)

Is that Mrs. Zooker out there?

RIGLEY (*removing his overcoat*)

Yes, she's talking with Mrs. Fox.

MARY (*hurriedly taking the book over to the little table at the left of the mantelpiece*)

Are they coming in?

RIGLEY

Mrs. Zooker is, immediately, yes; she has one of my lists.

[*Hangs his overcoat on the hall-tree.*

MARY

Well, you haven't been standing out there in the cold, have you?

RIGLEY

I should say I haven't!

MARY (*coming back towards the hall door*)

Well, listen, Loring!

RIGLEY (*coming in through the hall door, rubbing his hands*)

It's gotten fearfully cold!

[*Mr. Rigley is a baldheaded blond, with a slightly pedantic manner of speech, and a dignity, at all times, far in excess of even the dignity of his calling. He is a trifle stout for his forty years, although the clerical garb is not unbecoming to him. He wears black, heavy-rimmed nose-glasses with a black tape over his right ear.*

MARY (*handing him the telegram*)

This telegram came a few minutes ago; and I've been terribly anxious till you'd get here.

[*She touches an electric button at the right of the mantel-piece, and the room becomes illuminated — by means of the floor lamp over at the left. Then she starts across the room towards the window.*

RIGLEY

Is it for me?

MARY

No, it's for me.

RIGLEY

Bad news?

MARY

No, it's from my brother Joe!

RIGLEY (*reading the telegram*)

Eugene What?

MARY (*coming back to him*)

Eugene Tesh. He's that boy you've heard me speak of that used to go to school with my brother Joe and me — back in Baltimore; we used to live next door to each other when we were children.

RIGLEY

What's this, — "plays Youngstown the twenty-ninth"?

MARY

Yes, that's to-night; that's the reason I've been so

anxious till you'd get here. (*Looking over his left shoulder, and indicating a line with a finger of her left hand*) You see it says, "played Newark two weeks ago." (*To Rigley*) And Joe must have seen him; because it says, (*indicating the telegram again*) "Asked about you — told him you were living in Youngstown — gave him your address — he is going to walk in on you when he plays Youngstown the twenty-seventh — thought I'd better tip you off." (*She straightens up and looks at Rigley*) And, you see, to-day is the twenty-seventh!

RIGLEY (*with a puzzled expression*)

What does it mean, — he "*plays* Youngstown"?

MARY

He's on the stage! (*Rigley turns and looks at her as though she had just told him that she had decided to go on the stage herself*) He went on the stage shortly after he left school; it must be fifteen years ago.

RIGLEY

You mean that he is an actor?

MARY

Yes! — You've surely heard me speak of Eugene Tesh!

RIGLEY (*handing her back the telegram with a touch of state, as he passes in front of her and proceeds towards the little table at the left of the mantelpiece*)

I can't say that I have.

MARY

Well, his name is always in the newspapers; he's a dramatic star.

RIGLEY (*picking up the black book and opening it, with a suggestion of ceremony*)

I am not familiar with the names of dramatic stars.

MARY

I thought perhaps you might have seen his name on one of the theatrical bill-boards.

RIGLEY

I never look at theatrical bill-boards.

MARY (*coming a little forward at the right of the center table*)

I suppose Joe thought he'd better send me this wire so that I'd be sure and be in, in case Mr. Tesh comes.

RIGLEY (*closing the book, with a rather uninvolved expression*)

Well, you can be in if you like.

[*He looks at her, and she meets the look; then he starts for the door at the left.*

MARY (*taking a step or two towards him*)

Well, you'll see him if he comes, won't you, Loring?

[*He stops and turns to her, then comes back a step or two.*

RIGLEY

Isn't that rather a strange question to ask me?

MARY

Why so?

RIGLEY

You understand the opposition of our church to the theater?

MARY

But, this isn't the theater, Loring!

RIGLEY

Your friend is of it, isn't he?

MARY

Yes, of course.

RIGLEY

Very well, then. Besides, I think I have sufficiently emphasized my *personal* opposition to the theater; the life of the stage is not compatible with the life of a

Christian, and I see nothing to be gained by association with its people.

MARY

Well, what can I do?

RIGLEY

You can do nothing very well, under the circumstances; but I *certainly* shouldn't care to have any of the members know that we were entertaining stage folk.

MARY

They needn't know anything about it.

RIGLEY

How could you prevent it, if he should walk in while Mrs. Zooker is here. (*He looks at his watch*)   What time is he coming?

MARY

It doesn't say in this wire.

RIGLEY

It's eight minutes past five now.

MARY (*glancing at the clock on the mantelpiece*)

Well, if he has to play to-night, I don't see how he's going to come out here, unless he comes before dinner.

RIGLEY (*replacing his watch, and starting for the door at the left*)

Tell Mrs. Zooker to bring her list right into the study. (*He reaches the door and stops*)   And-a- (*He turns to Mary*)   If it should be necessary to introduce your friend to her, I should suggest that you refer to him as an acquaintance, rather than as an actor.   And let me know when he's gone. (*Mary looks at him steadily; he turns and starts through the door*)   You'd better put something around your shoulders — this room isn't any too warm.

[*Mary stands for a second irresolute; then, suddenly,*

*starts to follow him; but the voice of Mrs. Zooker in the
hallway — at the right — arrests her; so she replaces the
telegram in the bosom of her dress and stands looking at
the hall door.*

MRS. ZOOKER (*in the hallway*)

If you'll wait there for a second I'll call her. (*Appearing at the door leading into the hallway*) Why, there's a gentleman here to see you, Mrs. Rigley.

MARY

Oh, is there, Mrs. Zooker?

MRS. ZOOKER (*sidling in, and standing a little to the right of the door*)

Yes, he's right out here at the door.

MARY (*glancing in the mirror over the mantelpiece, and touching her hair and dress*)

Thanks, so much. Mr. Rigley said to go right into the study.

MRS. ZOOKER (*starting across towards the door at the left*)

Oh, all right, I will.

MARY (*going out through the hall door*)

Aren't you frozen?

MRS. ZOOKER

No, I don't seem to mind the cold very much.

MARY

You're lucky! (*Speaking to Tesh at the front door*) Is this Eugene Tesh?

[*Mrs. Zooker, who is just leaving the room through the door
at the left, pauses, and tiptoes back to the left of the mantelpiece; from which point she endeavors, by dint of divers
peerings and strainings, to see what is going on at the front
door.*

[*She's a poor old thing, this Mrs. Zooker, with a wizened*

*little face and no teeth; and a get-up generally that is
redolent of rummage sales and vanished vogues. She wears
a skimpy coat of faded black — three-quarter length —
and a heavy gray skirt, quite full, and touching all the way
around. Her hat is black — a little toque, rather rusty,
and trimmed with a dab of withered violets, from whose
center looms the remnant of a saffron-colored ostrich tip.
She has a very ratty muff, of nameless fur, depending on
a soiled and knotted cord; and, around her neck, she wears
a stringy scarf, one end of which is thrown back over her
shoulder.*

TESH (*at the front door*)

Then, you have been expecting me?

MARY

Only for the past fifteen minutes. I'm so glad to see
you again, Gene!

TESH

And I am certainly delighted to see you too, Mary!

MARY

You certainly have grown up!

[*At the approach of the voices, Mrs. Zooker scurries
through the door at the left.*

TESH

So have you!

MARY (*laughing, and appearing at the hall door; hanging
Tesh's hat on the hall-tree*)

Have I?

TESH

Rather!

[*The front door closes.*

MARY (*coming into the room*)

Come right in, Gene. (*After taking a few steps forward*

and to the left, she stops, and faces the hall door. Tesh appears; and takes the room in at a glance) I suppose we've been thinking of each other as we were at school.

TESH

Yes.

[*He starts down towards the center table.*

[*He is a dramatic star, of considerable reputation, with a personality possessing that quality which has been defined as stellar. He is tall and thin, — has a lot of soft-looking black hair and is rather austerely pale; although this latter characteristic is somewhat nullified by a certain charm of manner, and the suggestion of a twinkle in his eye. He wears a long, beautifully tailored coat of excellent black, with a high, rolling collar; and, under it, a perfectly cut, double-breasted sack suit of the same material. He is quietly gloved and spatted; wears a gorgeous shawl scarf of steel-blue silk around his neck, and carries a snakewood cane, tipped with silver.*

MARY

I had this wire from Joe only fifteen minutes ago, saying that you were to play here to-night; otherwise I don't suppose I should *ever* have known that you were in town at all.

TESH (*standing just above the center table*)

I had intended to walk in on you and surprise you.

MARY

Well, you certainly have!

TESH (*removing his gloves and tossing them on the table*)

But Joe has given it away.

[*He leans over to look at a small framed photograph on the table.*

MARY (*standing to the left of the center table*)

Well, I suppose he only did that to make sure that I'd be in, so that you wouldn't have your trip out here for nothing. Won't you take off your things, Gene?

TESH (*lifting his cane from his left arm*)

I'll take off my cane.

MARY (*laughing a little, and indicating the back of the armchair at the right of the center table*)

Put it there.

TESH (*holding the cane toward her*)

You see I carry a cane now.

MARY

So I see. Is that the sign of age?

TESH (*turning to her, after having hung the cane on the back of the armchair*)

Sign of an actor. You seem to be very nicely fixed here, Mary.

MARY

Yes, we're comfortable.

TESH

Joe tells me you married a minister.

MARY

Yes; Doctor Rigley.

TESH

How do you like him? (*Checking himself*) I mean, do you get along well with him?

MARY

Yes; very well.

TESH

You do?

MARY

Yes.

TESH (*commencing to remove his coat*)

I've never been in a minister's house before.

MARY

Haven't you?

TESH

No; it's quite like other people's houses, isn't it?

MARY

You're quite like other people, Gene.

[*He laughs.*

TESH

You wouldn't have thought so if you'd seen the way that old woman stared at me out at the door.

[*He folds his coat over the back of the armchair.*

MARY

Who, Mrs. Zooker?

TESH (*removing his scarf*)

The old woman that let me in.

MARY

Yes, that's Mrs. Zooker.

TESH

Does she work here?

MARY (*coming forward to the chair at the left of the center table*)

No, she just helps my husband with the church work. Sit down, Gene.

TESH (*placing the scarf across the back of the chair, and moving around to the front of the chair*)

I can't stay a moment, Mary; my train was two hours late.

MARY (*sitting at the left of the table*)

Did you just get into town?

TESH (*sitting at the right of the table*)

Ten minutes ago; I came out here in a taxi.

MARY

Well, you can sit down for a minute.

TESH

I haven't been to a hotel yet.

MARY (*resting her elbows on the table*)

And, what have you been doing all these years, Gene?

TESH (*picking up the little framed photograph from the table*)

Acting, all over the place. Is this your husband's picture?

MARY

No, that's Abraham Lincoln.

TESH (*setting down the picture, and picking up a little black book*)

And, what sort of a man is your husband, Mary?

MARY

Oh, like most ministers, I suppose.

TESH

But, I don't know any ministers. What book is this?

MARY

That's our church manual.

TESH

Very interesting, I suppose?

MARY

If you're a good church member.

TESH (*putting it down on the table, as he rises*)

I'll have to get a copy.

[*Mary laughs a little, and rises also.*

MARY

I suppose you never go to church, do you, Gene?

TESH (*coming forward, as though he were approaching a window*)

No, but I have a very intimate friend who has been there. Is this your church out here?

MARY

Yes; don't you think it's pretty?

TESH (*nodding his head slowly*)

Hum-hum. I should say romantic.

MARY

Rather; we had three weddings in it last month.

TESH (*casually*)

It isn't so innocent as it looks, is it?

MARY

Are you married, Gene?

TESH (*turning to her suddenly*)

What?

MARY

I say, are you married?

TESH

Why, not this season.

[*He resumes his observation of the church.*

MARY (*turning away from him, laughing*)

You're perfectly dreadful, Gene! (*Turning back to him*) Aren't you really married, Gene?

TESH

No, really, I'm not, Mary.

MARY

Why, I thought you'd have been married years ago.

TESH (*raising his hand in disapproval, and passing across her towards the window at the left*)

I shouldn't care for it.

MARY (*crossing over back of the center table, and moving down to the right of it*)

Well, how do you know whether you would or not?

TESH

I have played husbands so often that I am quite dis-
illusioned.

MARY

Are you playing the part of a husband in this piece
you're doing now?

TESH

Yes; he's one of those very good husbands; I'll be
glad when the season is over. (*Coming away from
the window*)   By the way, Mary, — where is *your*
husband?

MARY

In his study, I believe.

TESH

Does he know I'm here?

MARY

I haven't told him.

TESH

Going to?

MARY (*rather embarrassed, and smiling*)

Not necessarily, Gene.

[*He stops, inclines his head and raises his eyebrows comprehendingly.*

TESH

Is he opposed to the theater?

MARY

Very much; our church is, you know.

TESH

Oh, really?   Are you?

MARY

Indeed, I'm not!   (*Tesh laughs*)   I'm crazy about the
theater, and always have been.

TESH

Well, do you go?

MARY

I can't very well; he's so dreadfully opposed, personally.

TESH (*glancing over his shoulder towards the door at the
left*)

I suppose it's a lucky thing Mrs. Zooker didn't know
that I was an actor a while ago, or she wouldn't have
let me in at all.

MARY

I guess not. But, really, Gene, I haven't been to see a
play since I've been married; and that's nearly seven
years ago.

TESH (*sitting on the edge of the table*)

Oh, dear me!

MARY

Can you imagine that!

TESH

No.

MARY

And you were playing in New York three years ago,
while we were there —

TESH

Is that so?

MARY

Yes; and I did my level best to try and get to see you;
but I simply couldn't manage it; and it nearly broke
my heart, because I've always been dying to see you
on the stage.

TESH

Well, we must try and manage it to-night, Mary.

MARY

I don't think we'll succeed. (*Tesh thinks keenly for a second, then glances towards the door at the left*)

TESH

Has your husband ever been on the stage?

MARY

Heavens, no!

TESH

You should have told him that he ought to have been; it invariably removes any prejudices.

MARY (*very much amused*)

I'm afraid he'd shoot me, Gene!

TESH

Hah! Not the slightest danger, my dear girl; that is the flattering word; the one compliment that has never failed. Tell any man, woman or child that he should be on the stage, — and you'll find him quite as susceptible as a cat is to catnip.

MARY

Why is that, Gene?

TESH

Because every human being has, at some time or other in his life, experienced the desire to be on the stage. Of course, he may not admit it; but he has, just the same; and if he hasn't, all you've got to do is tell him he should be on the stage, and he *will* experience it. (*She laughs*) I tell you, Mary, that is the universal susceptibility. And very naturally so; the most fundamental instinct of human life is to express oneself; and the stage is perhaps the most complete form of self-expression; so that — when a person is stage-struck — he is simply struck with the desire to express himself more

completely. If I were to tell Mrs. Zooker — or your
husband — or anybody — from the minister to the
mechanic — that he should be on the stage — why —
the first thing you know he'd start inquiring about the
fare to New York.

MARY (*laughing a little, and going up to the mantelpiece*)

Well, please don't tell my husband or Mrs. Zooker that
they should have been on the stage while I'm in the room.

TESH

Why not?

MARY (*coming down at his left, carrying a little old-fashioned
photograph in a black frame, which she has taken from the
mantelpiece*)

Because I'd never be able to keep my face straight.
(*Tesh laughs*) Here's a little picture of my husband;
it's ages old, but it isn't a bad picture. He had it taken
in Boston I think, a long time ago.

TESH

Does he look like this?

MRS. ZOOKER (*sidling through the door at the left*)

You'll have to excuse me for bothering you, Mrs. Rigley —

[*Mrs. Rigley turns, and Tesh rises.*

MARY

Oh, are you going, Mrs. Zooker?

MRS. ZOOKER (*crossing towards the door leading into the
hallway*)

Yes, I've got to run along; it's after five. I told Mr.
Rigley I'd be right over again after supper, to go over
that other list.

[*She has reached the hall door, and Tesh has moved slowly
towards the left.*

MARY

Oh, Mrs. Zooker! (*Mrs. Zooker turns*) I want you to meet Mr. Tesh. (*Tesh turns. Mrs. Zooker melts and shrinks, as Mary puts her arm around her waist and leads her slowly down to the right of the center table, talking as she comes*) This is a boy that I went to school with in Baltimore, nearly fifteen years ago.

MRS. ZOOKER

Oh, is that a fact, Mrs. Rigley!

MARY

And we haven't seen each other since. Mrs. Zooker, Gene.

TESH (*advancing very graciously, and crossing to the right in front of the center table*)

How do you do, Mrs. Zooker?

MRS. ZOOKER

I'm pleased to meet you, I'm sure.

TESH

Thank you.

MRS. ZOOKER (*looking straight ahead*)

You're welcome.

[*Tesh glances at her; then, after half-glancing over his left shoulder in the direction of Mary, who has gradually come down on the left of the center table, and is arranging the photograph of Abraham Lincoln, he turns back to Mrs. Zooker.*

TESH

What company are you here with, Mrs. Zooker?

[*Mary looks up suddenly.*

MRS. ZOOKER

Sir?

TESH

I say, what company are you playing here with?

MARY (*laying her hand on Tesh's arm*)

Gene, Mrs. Zooker isn't on the stage!

TESH

Beg pardon?

MARY

I say, Mrs. Zooker isn't on the stage.

TESH (*turning back to Mrs. Zooker in polite surprise*)

Oh, isn't she?

MARY

No.

TESH (*turning slowly to Mary*)

Why, I thought I understood you to say that Mrs. Zooker was in the profession?

MARY

No, I didn't, Gene.

TESH (*turning back to Mrs. Zooker, rather amused*)

Well, how extraordinary that I should have gotten that impression! (*He laughs faintly; and Mrs. Zooker, not knowing what else to do, laughs a little too; then Tesh turns back to Mary*) I was quite sure you said that Mrs. Zooker was in the profession.

[*But Mary has slipped across back of him towards Mrs. Zooker.*

MRS. ZOOKER

What's he sayin'?

MARY (*placing her hand on Mrs. Zooker's arm*)

Mr. Tesh thought you were an actress, dear.

MRS. ZOOKER

Who, me?

MARY

Yes.

MRS. ZOOKER (*turning suddenly away from Mary, to the right*)

Good night! (*She breaks into a cackling, self-conscious laugh, and goes up to the hall door; and Mary crosses down to the extreme right. Mrs. Zooker turns at the hall door and speaks directly to Mary*) I'll have to tell our Lena that!

MARY

Yes, you must.

MRS. ZOOKER (*coming slowly forward again at the right of the table*)

I'm sure I don't know what there is about me that'd make anybody think that! (*She laughs again*) Oh, dear! — What made you think it, Mr. Tesh?

TESH

What did you say, Mrs. Zooker?

MRS. ZOOKER

I say, — what made you think I was an actress?

TESH

Well, I don't know that I could say exactly, Mrs. Zooker, but, — well, you gave me that impression.

MRS. ZOOKER

Is that a fact?

TESH

Yes.

MRS. ZOOKER (*turning to Mary*)

What do you think of that! (*She laughs again; then settles her muff*) I guess it must have been my voice.

TESH

It may have been.

MRS. ZOOKER

Because I know when I was growing up, — people always used to say that I had quite a voice.

TESH

Well, you have appeared publicly, haven't you?

MRS. ZOOKER (*becoming a bit serious*)

Well, not much these late years; but before I was married I used to go on quite a bit —

TESH (*raising his finger*)

Ah!

MRS. ZOOKER

At the little affairs we used to have at the Sunday school.

TESH

You recited, didn't you?

MRS. ZOOKER

Yes.

TESH

Dramatic recitations?

MRS. ZOOKER

Very dramatic.

TESH

I should imagine you would do those best.

MRS. ZOOKER

Is that so?

TESH

Yes, — there is a distinctly dramatic quality in your voice, Mrs. Zooker.

MRS. ZOOKER

Is that a fact?

TESH

Distinctly.

MRS. ZOOKER (*turning to Mary and breaking into a laugh*)

Now, what do you think of that! (*Turning back to Tesh*) Well, now, that's a funny thing, because since I've been married, I've kinda give it up.

TESH

Ah, don't you think that was a mistake, Mrs. Zooker?

MRS. ZOOKER

Well, yes, I do, sometimes, Mr. Tesh; but, you see, my husband has always carried on so, whenever I've went on.

TESH

I see, I see.

MRS. ZOOKER

Of course, he has no talent of any kind hisself, so I don't suppose he can understand how anybody else can have any.

[*She nods rather vigorously at the conclusion of this remark, and Tesh joins her in the nodding.*

TESH

Yes, that's the way it goes, Mrs. Zooker.

MRS. ZOOKER

But, do you know, it's a funny thing, Mr. Tesh! — It just seems like the Irony of Fate — I have a daughter —

TESH

Ah, yes?

MRS. ZOOKER (*turning to Mary*)

Our Lena — (*Mary smiles and nods*) Mrs. Rigley here has heard her — she'll be fifteen the twenty-first day of this coming May; and, do you know, she just seems to have *took* that from me.

TESH

You mean, her talent?

MRS. ZOOKER

Yes! (*Tesh nods comprehendingly*) Now, last Thanksgiving Eve — (*checking herself*) No, I'm telling a lie; it was New Year's Eve.

TESH

I was going to say —

MRS. ZOOKER

We were having a little entertainment down at the Guild; and she done that piece of Longfellow's, called, "Ring the Bells" —

TESH

Ah, yes, yes!

MRS. ZOOKER

And, do you know, she was just wonderful, really! And as I sat there watchin' her, goin' through her gestures, and takin' her part off so good, — I just began to realize what a fool I'd been to give it all up. (*Tesh appreciates her tragedy, with a slow, serious nod*) And I made up my mind, then and there (*turning to Mary*) that if our Lena's cut out for the stage, — I'll never raise my voice to keep her from it!

TESH

You're a very sensible woman, Mrs. Zooker.

MRS. ZOOKER

Never! She can go to the heights, (*with a dramatic gesture*) and I'll never stand in her way!

[*The clock strikes five-thirty.*

TESH

You're a very sensible woman.

MRS. ZOOKER (*turning abruptly to Mary*)

Well, I've got to run along — it's half-past five! (*She starts for the hall door, then remembers and steps back to Tesh*) Well, I'm awful glad to have met you, Mr. Tesh, I'm sure.

TESH (*taking her hand*)

Thank you, Mrs. Zooker; I'm sure I'm very pleased to have met you, too.

MRS. ZOOKER (*holding his hand*)

I'm goin' to ast you an awful personal question, if it wouldn't be makin' too free?

TESH (*smiling*)

Not at all, what is it?

MRS. ZOOKER

Ain't you an actor?

TESH

Yes.

MRS. ZOOKER (*turning suddenly to Mary*)

Now, ain't that funny! I never set eyes on Mr. Tesh before in all my life; and yet, the minute I seen you at the door, I knowed you was an actor!

TESH (*amused*)

Well, you know the old saying, Mrs. Zooker, "The eagle knows the eagle."

MRS. ZOOKER (*breaking into a laugh*)

Well, I guess there's somethin' in that, too!

TESH

Indeed, I guess there is. (*He turns away slightly to hide his amusement*) Yes, indeed.

MRS. ZOOKER

My husband has been an eagle for twelve years. (*Tesh moves to the window at the left*) Well, I've got to skip along. (*She goes up to the hall door and turns again. Mary has crossed back of her to the mantelpiece*) Do you show here to-night, Mr. Tesh?

TESH (*turning from the window*)

Yes.

MRS. ZOOKER

How do you like Youngstown?

TESH

Oh, it's like New York, and the rest of them.

MRS. ZOOKER

Well, of course, we don't think there's no place in the world like Youngstown.

TESH

I've never seen anything just like it.

MRS. ZOOKER

I'm sorry Mr. Tesh couldn't have met our Lena.

MARY

Yes, it's too bad.

TESH

Is she the one who recites?

MRS. ZOOKER

Yes; she's not home this afternoon, or I'd have her come over, and do one or two of her little pieces for you.

TESH

That'd be lovely.

MRS. ZOOKER

She went to that lecture at the Guild.

MARY

Oh, did she?

MRS. ZOOKER

Yes; and I'm kinda anxious till she gets home to hear how it was. Good-by, Mr. Tesh.

TESH

Good-by, Mrs. Zooker.

MRS. ZOOKER

I guess my husband'll think I've eloped. (*She laughs, and they join her, out of courtesy; then she hurries out into the hallway. Mary stops at the hall door, and stands looking into the hallway after her, — and Tesh takes a walk down around the settee and up again to the left-hand corner of the mantelpiece*) Now, don't come out here in this cold hallway with me!

MARY

I won't.

MRS. ZOOKER

That's the way people gets their death. I'll let myself out.

MARY

All right, Mrs. Zooker. (*The outer door is heard to close. Mary turns and looks at Tesh, then goes down to the right of the center table, laughing*) You're perfectly terrible, Gene!

TESH (*suddenly, and starting down at the left of the table towards her*)

Listen! You don't think there's any danger of her bringing her daughter over here, do you?

MARY

I don't think she's home.

TESH

You know, I've heard a few child wonders in my time.
[*Rigley appears at the left door.*

MARY (*seeing him over Tesh's shoulder, and starting up towards the mantelpiece*)

What is it, Loring?

RIGLEY

Has Mrs. Zooker gone?

MARY

Yes, this minute; did you want to see her?

RIGLEY (*crossing in front of her to the hall door*)

I did, yes; but it's unimportant; she'll be over again this evening.

MARY

Yes, she said she would. (*Mr. Rigley glances out into the hallway, then turns and recrosses the room, giving Tesh a penetrating and disapproving look as he goes. Tesh, however, is occupied with an examination of the little photograph, which he still holds in his hands. Just as Rigley reaches the door at the left, Mary calls him*) Oh, Loring! (*He stops, and turns to her*) I want you to meet Mr. Tesh. (*Tesh turns quietly and rests his fingers on the center table*) This is the Eugene Tesh that you've possibly heard me speak of — that I used to go to school with in Baltimore (*turning to Tesh and half laughing*) I'm ashamed to say how many years ago. My husband, Gene.

TESH (*inclining his head pleasantly*)

How do you do, Mr. Rigley?

RIGLEY

How do you do, sir?

TESH

I should have known you from your photograph.

MARY

I've just been showing Mr. Tesh that old picture you had taken in Boston.

RIGLEY

That's quite an old picture.

TESH

Taken before you entered the ministry, wasn't it, Mr. Rigley?

RIGLEY (*coming forward a little*)

Oh, yes, yes.

TESH

I noticed you weren't wearing the frock.

MARY

I've always been trying to persuade him to have some new pictures taken, but he simply won't do it.

RIGLEY

That's quite a good picture.

MARY

But it's ages old, Loring! And, besides, it isn't very ministerial-looking, either. Now, if I didn't know you, and were to see that picture, I'd be more likely to think it was the picture of a well-to-do business man than a minister. (*Tesh laughs deprecatingly*) Wouldn't you, Gene?

TESH

No, I should hardly say a business man.

MARY

Well, you'd never say a minister, would you?

TESH

No, I don't think I should.

MARY

Now, you see that, Loring!

TESH (*looking at the picture, with his head a bit on one side*)

I'm afraid I'd be more inclined to think it might be the picture of an actor.

[*There is a slight pause. Mary turns away smoothly, touching her hair, and moves over towards the right; and her husband, looking over his glasses at Tesh, begins to melt, very visibly. Then he sways towards Tesh, breaking into a very orthodox little chuckle.*

RIGLEY (*taking the photograph*)

That's very funny.

TESH

I daresay Mr. Rigley will be very much scandalized, but — really —

RIGLEY

No, — you're not the first that said that.

TESH (*glancing at Mary, who has come down to the right of the center table and is standing on a line with him*)

No?

RIGLEY

My photographs invariably give that impression.

TESH

Is that so?

RIGLEY

Invariably.

TESH

Then, there must be some truth in it, Mr. Rigley.

RIGLEY (*vastly pleased*)

Well, "what everybody says", you know!

[*He bursts into delighted laughter.*

TESH (*laughing with him*)

Indeed, that's very true!

[*As Mr. Rigley's laughter continues, Tesh glances at Mary, and she looks away.*

RIGLEY

You know, Mr. Tesh, it's a most extraordinary thing — that nine out of ten persons who see this photograph, are of the impression that it is the photograph of a dramatic artist.

TESH

Yes?

RIGLEY

And, personally, I have never been able to understand why that should be so.

TESH

Well, frankly, Mr. Rigley, I can't see how anybody who

would be at all familiar with the dramatic earmarks —
could come to any other conclusion.

RIGLEY

Is that so?

TESH

Take this line here, for example.

RIGLEY (*looking closely*)

You mean —

TESH

From the tip of your nose to the top of your upper
lip.

RIGLEY

Yes, yes, I see what you mean!

TESH

That line is essentially dramatic.

RIGLEY

Is that so?

TESH

Essentially.   Then, of course, the eye is an unfailing
indication.

RIGLEY (*looking closely at the picture*)

I don't know that I have ever noticed the eye particularly.   Excuse me just a moment, till I get my other
glasses!

TESH

That's quite all right.

RIGLEY (*hurrying to the mantelpiece, removing his nose
glasses and putting them into a breast-pocket case as he
goes*)

It's rather difficult to see anything very closely with
these.

[*Tesh glances at Mary significantly.*

TESH

Mr. Rigley, have you ever seen a photograph of Edwin Booth?

RIGLEY (*picking up a pair of enormous, rimmed spectacles from the mantelpiece, and settling them on his nose*)

Edwin Booth, the actor, you mean?

TESH

Yes.

RIGLEY (*coming forward*)

Yes, I believe I have, Mr. Tesh.

TESH

Didn't anything strike you particularly?

RIGLEY

About Mr. Booth's picture, you mean?

TESH

Yes.

RIGLEY

Well, really, it's been so long ago, I would scarcely remember.

TESH

Well, the next time you have an opportunity of seeing a photograph of Mr. Booth, I'd like you to compare it, right in around the eyes, with your picture here — right in here (*He points to a certain spot on the picture, which Rigley is still holding*) — see if you don't get what I mean.

[*He passes in front of Rigley and continues over towards the left; while Mary moves from her position at the right up towards the mantelpiece. Mr. Rigley, however, remains perfectly still, looking intently at his photograph.*

MRS. ZOOKER (*in the hallway out at the right*)

Here we come right in, without ringing! (*Appearing at*

*the hall door, and speaking back over her shoulder to Lena,
who is evidently out at the street door)* Close that door,
dear! *(To Mary)* I thought I'd like to have Lena
meet Mr. Tesh! *(To Mr. Rigley, who has turned from
his contemplation of the photograph and is looking at her
rather grandly)* Excuse me, Doctor. *(Rigley inclines
his head, a bit condescendingly, and passes over in front
of the table to the right, where he resumes his study of the
picture)* Hurry, Lena! *(Addressing Mrs. Rigley, as
she comes into the room and takes up her position just to the
left of the door)* I didn't think she'd be home from the
lecture yet, but she sez it was over before five. *(Lena
has straggled in during this last speech, and comes forward
a few steps, when her eye lights upon Tesh; she stops
dead, and looks at him steadily and appraisingly; and
he looks at her in puzzled curiosity. Mrs. Zooker stands
looking from one to the other very affably. Presently,
she takes Lena by the arm and addresses herself to
Tesh)* This is the girl I was speakin' to you about
— our Lena.

[*Tesh advances a step or two, and Mary passes above him,
and goes down to the left of the settee.*

TESH *(bowing very graciously)*

How do you do, Lena?

LENA *(casually)*

Hello.

[*Lena, as her mother has already observed, will be fifteen
the twenty-first of this coming May. And she looks it;
except for — perhaps just a bit too much bust — if one
may so say. But then Lena is "perhaps just a bit too
much" all over. And no wonder; for she's forever eating.
Something. Always chewing. One of those little fatties*

*that doesn't care where she is or how she looks, so long as
there's refreshments. And it's very possible that "how she
looks" is of even less concern to her than "where she is";
for she's been wearing the same coat for the last five years.
And it's a very dirty coat too — by this time — naturally.
A gray-green — long ago outgrown, and without a button.
But Lena doesn't mind that. She never gets cold. She
just gets red — the color of her hat. A little pot hat of rose-
colored felt, much too narrow for the width of Lena's face,
and trimmed with a buckle of pea-green patent leather, and
a brief, frightened-looking little quill in the same shade.
The hat is secured by a broad, extremely tight-looking strap
of black elastic under the chin. Incidentally, Lena is just
about at an age when she can wear her mother's shoes, and,
at present, she appears to be taking advantage of the pos-
sibility. Not with the most complete success, however, as
the shoes, an old brown pair, with tan-cloth tops, have,
owing to the weakness of Lena's ankles, turned in and out
respectively; an effect which is scarcely improved by the
absence of the tongue of the right shoe and the consequent
glimpse of the white stocking between the laces. When the
coat is removed, there is revealed a washed-out middy blouse
with a bow of broad red ribbon fastened with a ten-cent
brooch — instead of the customary tie-effect — and a wide,
black, patent leather belt around her waist. There is also
a knee-length skirt of crimson satine, trimmed with two
folds of itself near the bottom. Her hair is swept back from
her face, rather than combed, and the short ends on top are
tied with a little bow of red ribbon at the back of her head.
The removal of her hat discloses perhaps the only surviving
specimen of the old-fashioned circular back comb. And
the heavy tan mittens have a past, too.*

MRS. ZOOKER (*snatching Lena's hat off, and rushing over to put it on the buffet at the right*)

Mr. Tesh is an actor, dear; and I thought if you'd just run over one or two of them little pieces that you done New Year's Eve at the Guild, it might give him an idea of your talent. (*Running back and dragging Lena's coat off*) You remember that piece you done New Year's Eve, don't you?

LENA (*disinterestedly*)

I done two pieces New Year's Eve.

MRS. ZOOKER

Yes, I know; but I mean the first one you done, — when they clapped you so; about ringin' the bells?

LENA

Oh, that was "Ring Out Wild Bells", by Alfred G. Tennyson.

MRS. ZOOKER

Yes, that's the one I mean. (*Speaking to Tesh, as she crosses to place the coat on the armchair in front of the fireplace*) I don't think Mr. Tesh has ever heard that, have you, Mr. Tesh?

TESH

I don't believe I have, Mrs. Zooker.

MRS. ZOOKER (*settling the collar of Lena's blouse*)

It's an awful dramatic thing, but I guess that's right in your line, ain't it?

TESH (*smiling*)

Quite so.

MRS. ZOOKER (*guiding Lena to the center of the room*)

Now, stand right there, dear, and do that for Mr. Tesh.

LENA

I don't think I remember it any more!

MRS. ZOOKER

Well, say what you remember, dear.

LENA (*to Tesh*)

I ain't spoke it since New Year's.

MRS. ZOOKER

Well, it'll come to you as you go along; (*turning to Tesh*) and I'm sure Mr. Tesh won't mind, even if you do break down.

TESH

That's quite all right.

MARY

Sit here, Gene.

[*He sits down on the settee, and Mary remains standing at the left.*

MRS. ZOOKER (*backing away from Lena, to the right*)

Now, stand right up straight, dear; and don't forget your gestures.

RIGLEY (*for Tesh's benefit*)

Try and get the full, round tone, Lena.

[*He glances at Tesh, and then looks straight ahead.*

LENA

Yes, sir. (*Tesh turns and looks at Mary, then waits for Lena to begin. She is busy, however, with the work of taking off her mittens, and, presently, Tesh turns to see the cause of the delay. There is an end of lace — probably, from her petticoat or pants — hanging below the hem of her skirt; and Tesh becomes conscious of it. Immediately Lena comprehends the object of his attention and tries to remedy the condition by pulling down her skirt. Then Tesh turns away, and, looking straight ahead, awaits the ordeal. Lena extends her mittens towards her mother*)

Hold these.

[*Mrs. Zooker advances, takes them, and resumes her place. Tesh has turned to see the nature of this last postponement, and again resumes his attitude of resignation.*

MRS. ZOOKER (*as Lena continues to prepare*)

Go on, dear.

LENA (*holding the sides of her skirt with both hands, and breaking into a faint, flat voice*)

> "Ring out, wild bells, to the wild sky,
> The flying cloud, the frosty light;
> The year is dying in the night;
> Ring out, wild bells, and let him die."

MRS. ZOOKER

Louder, dear! (*Tesh turns and looks at Mrs. Zooker; so does Lena*) Louder.

LENA (*turning to resume, and speaking a little louder*)

> "Ring out the old, ring in the new —
> Ring, happy bells, across the snow;
> The year is going, let him go;"

(*Here Lena makes a kind of lunging gesture towards Tesh, which causes him to start slightly, and move quietly to the other end of the settee*)

> "Ring out the false, ring in the true."

[*The telephone bell rings twice.*

MRS. ZOOKER (*as Lena turns to her*)

Go right on, dear. (*To Mary, and starting towards the telephone at the left of the hall door*) I'll answer it! (*Picking up the telephone*) Go right on, Lena!

LENA

I forget where I was now!

MRS. ZOOKER

> "Ring out the grief that saps the mind,"

LENA (*turning to Tesh, smiling*)
Oh, sure!

> "Ring out the grief that saps the mind,
> For those that here we see no more;"

MRS. ZOOKER (*into the telephone*)
Mr. Who?
[*Tesh turns to Mary, but she is watching Mrs. Zooker.*
LENA

> "Ring out the feud of rich and poor,"

MRS. ZOOKER (*into the telephone*)
Magoon?
[*Rigley turns slowly and looks at Mrs. Zooker.*
LENA

> "Ring in redress to all mankind."

LENA and MRS. ZOOKER (*speaking at same time*)
{ (*Lena*) "Ring out a slowly dying cause,"
{ (*Mrs. Zooker, into the telephone*) Why, there's nobody
here by that name that I know of!
[*Tesh is in a still panic.*
LENA

> "And ancient forms of paltry strife;"

LENA and MRS. ZOOKER (*speaking at same time*)
{ (*Lena*) "Ring in the nobler modes of life,"
{ (*Mrs. Zooker*) Well just a minute, and I'll see!
LENA

> "With sweeter manners, purer laws."

LENA and MRS. ZOOKER (*speaking at same time*)
{ (*Lena*) "Ring out the care, the want, the sin,"
{ (*Mrs. Zooker, turning to Mr. Rigley*) There's a woman
here lookin' for a man called Magoon!

LENA and RIGLEY (*speaking at same time*)

{ (*Lena*) "The faithless coldness of the times;"
{ (*Rigley*) She must have the wrong number.

MRS. ZOOKER

She must have.

LENA

"Ring out, ring out, my mournful rhymes,"

LENA and MRS. ZOOKER (*speaking at same time*)

{ (*Lena*) "But ring the fuller minstrel in."
{ (*Mrs. Zooker, into the telephone*) Why, Mr. Rigley sez
you must have the wrong number.

LENA

"Ring out false pride in place of blood,"

MRS. ZOOKER (*into the telephone*)

This is Hillcrest, two four.

LENA

"The civic slander and the spite;"

MRS. ZOOKER (*into the telephone*)

You're welcome.

[*She sets down the telephone.*

LENA

"Ring in the love of truth and right,"

MRS. ZOOKER (*tiptoeing back to her place at Lena's right,
and speaking to Tesh and Mary as she goes*)

Excuse me.

LENA

"Ring in the common love of good."

[*Here she pauses, and, placing her hand to her mouth, turns
and looks at her mother.*

MRS. ZOOKER

Can't you remember the rest of it, dear?

LENA

No, I think that's all I remember just now; (*turning to Tesh*) it's been so long since I done it.

RIGLEY (*extending his arm magnificently, and breaking into declamation, as he struts across in front of the table towards Tesh*)

"Ring out old shapes of foul disease,"

RIGLEY and LENA (*speaking at same time*)

{ (*Rigley*) "Ring out the narrowing lust of gold;"
{ (*Lena, turning suddenly to her mother*) Oh, yes, I know what it is now!

MRS. ZOOKER

Shut up, dear!

RIGLEY (*becoming more dramatic as he proceeds*)

"Ring out

(*He makes a gesture here that comes rather close to Tesh's head*)

the thousand wars of old;

Ring in

(*He repeats the same sweeping gesture here, knocking Abraham Lincoln's picture off the center table*)

the thousand years of peace."

(*As the picture is knocked off the table, Mrs. Zooker utters a short screech, and rushes over to the right to pick it up. Rigley turns to Tesh*) How is that?

TESH (*applauding, in which Lena joins*)

Bravo, Mr. Rigley! Bravo!

[*Mrs. Zooker has picked up the photograph of Mr. Lincoln, and is giving it to Mary, who has crossed back of the settee to a point above the center table. As Mrs. Zooker hands Mary the picture, she makes a whispered comment to the effect of its not being broken, to which Mary nods, as she rearranges it on the table.*

RIGLEY

There's another verse or two, but they've escaped my mind.

[He goes up to the mantelpiece, shaking himself a bit, and laughing delightedly and self-consciously, and comes right down again.

TESH

I consider you a very great artist.

[Mr. Rigley lifts his hand deprecatingly, and, still laughing delightedly, turns, and goes up to the mirror over the mantelpiece and comes down again.

MRS. ZOOKER (*having come down at the right of the table, and crossing in front of it towards Tesh*)

See here, Mr. Rigley! (*Rigley turns to her, from the center of the room*) Mr. Tesh said a while ago that I ought to be on the stage!

RIGLEY

He was flattering you, Mrs. Zooker.

MRS. ZOOKER

Well, maybe he was; but I think he ought to tell you the same thing.

[Lena is still standing in the spot where she delivered her recitation; but, at this point, her eye rests upon Tesh's cane on the back of the armchair, and she moves towards it with the ostensible purpose of examining it more closely, but Mary, who is standing down at the right, observes her; and, anticipating her motive, steps to her side just as she is about to pick the cane up, and whispers that it might be safer to let it alone. Lena doesn't accept the suggestion with any too good grace, however; for, when Mary turns

*away, to resume her place, Lena turns on her heel with a
sneer, for canes in general, and wanders back towards the
settee.*

RIGLEY (*overflowing with deprecation, as he passes in front
of Tesh to the left*)

Oh, nonsense, Mrs. Zooker, nonsense!

MRS. ZOOKER

Don't you agree with me, Mr. Tesh?

TESH

Perfectly — perfectly — Mrs. Zooker! I'm afraid if
the pulpit hadn't gotten Mr. Rigley — the theater
would!

MRS. ZOOKER (*putting her arms around Lena, who has
wandered in at her left*)

But, what do you think of *my* little girl, Mr. Tesh?
[*Tesh turns and looks at Lena.*

TESH (*speaking very carefully*)

Why, Mrs. Zooker — I think if your daughter lives —
she has a future.

MRS. ZOOKER

Do you hear that, dear? (*Lena sneers and smiles, and
buries her face in her mother's shoulder*)
She does some comical pieces, too, but I guess she's forgotten them by this time, haven't you, dear? (*Lena
shakes her head affirmatively, still keeping her face in her
mother's shoulder*) Don't you remember that Irish
piece you used to do, about the cook? (*Lena shakes her
head negatively*) She used to do one of them pieces
where she had to take off the Irish brogue, — and she'd
have you dyin' in it.

TESH

I'd imagine she'd be delightful.

MRS. ZOOKER

You're sure you don't remember that piece, dear?

MARY (*coming a step or two forward from the right*)

Well, I'm afraid Mr. Tesh won't have much time, — if you want to be back in town by six.

TESH (*rising*)

Yes, I must go immediately. (*To Rigley, on his left*) I'm very sorry, Mr. Rigley.

[*Rigley bows.*

LENA (*standing right in his way, as he starts across to the back of the center table*)

Is that your automobile out there?

TESH

Yes.

LENA

Do you travel around in that?

MRS. ZOOKER (*brushing Lena out of Tesh's way*)

No, dear, he travels round on the trains. (*Tesh proceeds across to the center table and picks up his scarf and overcoat from the back of the armchair*) Where do you show to-morrow night, Mr. Tesh?

TESH

In — a — Akron, Ohio.

LENA

Where was you last night?

TESH

Erie. (*Handing his overcoat to Mary*) Please?

MRS. ZOOKER

P, A?

TESH

Yes.

MRS. ZOOKER

Oh, I'm sorry I didn't know! (*Addressing Lena*) He might have went out to see your Aunt Ida! (*Lena nods; and Tesh puts on his scarf and then gets into the coat that Mary is holding for him*) I have a sister living right outside of Erie — at Overbrooke.

TESH

Is that so?

MRS. ZOOKER

Yes; you might have went out to see her.

TESH

Yes, it's too bad I didn't know about it.

LENA

Where do you go after you go where you go to-morrow night?

TESH (*laughing*)

I think I shall have to send you my route, Lena.

MRS. ZOOKER (*coming forward at the left of the table, followed by Lena*)

Oh, Mr. Tesh! — do you know a young man by the name of Harry Culverson? (*Tesh comes down around the right of the table*) He's a distant relative of my husband's.

TESH

Why, I don't believe I do, Mrs. Zooker. Is he an actor?

MRS. ZOOKER

Oh, yes, he's right in your line; that's the reason I thought you might have run across him.

TESH

What company is he with?

MRS. ZOOKER

Why, the last letter we had from him, he had charge of the elephants, with the Barnum and Bailey Circus.

TESH

Well, I'm not very well acquainted among the elephants, Mrs. Zooker, I'm sorry to say.

LENA

Do you ever get ashamed when you first come out?

MRS. ZOOKER

She means nervous.

TESH

Oh, sometimes, yes.

MRS. ZOOKER

Lena does, too.

TESH

Is that so?

[*Mrs. Zooker nods.*

LENA

Is it true that Pearl White is the most beautiful woman in the world?

MRS. ZOOKER (*rather violently, and turning Lena towards the back, by the shoulder*)

Shut your mouth, Lena!

MARY (*taking a step or two to the buffet, where she leans*)

Don't forget your things, Gene.

TESH

No, I'm going immediately.

[*Lena crosses above the table and comes forward at Tesh's right.*

MRS. ZOOKER

I suppose you run across some awful funny people travelin' round the country the way you do, don't you, Mr. Tesh?

TESH

Yes, very funny indeed, Mrs. Zooker, — very funny.

LENA

How do you get your laundry done, when you're always on the go?

MRS. ZOOKER (*sharply*)

Don't ast so many questions, Lena! (*Lena gives her mother a withering look, then swishes a few steps to the right and slightly forward; then she stops, and makes a face of contempt for her mother. Tesh stands watching her; so does Mrs. Zooker*) Oh, there's a question I wanted to ast you, Mr. Tesh, before I forget it! Did you ever show in a place called Hutchinson, Kansas?

TESH

Hutchinson, Kansas? I believe I've passed through there several times.

MRS. ZOOKER

It's right outside of Dodge City.

TESH

Yes, I know where it is.

MRS. ZOOKER

Well, the reason I ast you, is 'cause we had a neighbor went out there to live some years ago, —

TESH

Oh, is that so?

MRS. ZOOKER

And she sent Lena the loveliest postal card of Niagara Falls. Lena saves them. (*Tesh turns and looks at Lena*) She has quite a collection. So, if ever you run across a very fancy one, she'd be delighted to have you send it to her, — wouldn't you, dear?

LENA

Sure.

TESH

Well, when I get back to New York, — I'll send her one of the — Rocky Mountains.

[*He starts to go, turning away from Mrs. Zooker to the right.*

LENA (*rather condescendingly, as Tesh smiles at her in passing*)

Thank you.

MARY

Have you everything, Gene?

TESH (*picking up his gloves from the table*)

I think so.

[*Mrs. Zooker moves up to the center of the room, and Lena follows her, crossing in front of the center table.*

MRS. ZOOKER

Well, Mr. Tesh, what do you think I ought to do about this girl? Do you think she belongs on the stage? — She's always acting!

LENA (*turning away, considerably embarrassed*)

Oh, I am not!

[*Tesh laughs, and looks at Mary, who reflects his amusement.*

MRS. ZOOKER

Now, you are too, dear!

TESH

There are very few of us who are *not* always acting, Mrs. Zooker; it's only when one learns how *not* to act, — that one really belongs on the stage.

MRS. ZOOKER

Well, what do you think I ought to do with her?

TESH

What are you doing with her now?

MRS. ZOOKER

Why, she's a waitress down in Schuster's Bakery —
on Fridays and Saturdays; but she's terrible dis-
satisfied; sez she'd much rather be in the Moving
Pictures.

TESH

Well, that isn't a bad idea; many waitresses have done
very well in the pictures. However — personally, I
think your daughter is a bit young to think of leaving
the Bakery.

MRS. ZOOKER

Well, I think that myself.

TESH (*casually picking up his cane from the back of the armchair*)

Besides, in a bakery, an actress can always be reasonably sure of getting something to eat.

MRS. ZOOKER

Yes, that's true enough.

TESH

However, — if her genius continues to develop, — I
think it would not be a bad idea to take her to see a play
occasionally.

MRS. ZOOKER (*a trifle disconcerted*)

Well, of course, we don't go to the theater very much
— on account of the church being opposed, you
know.

TESH

Is your church opposed to the theater?

MRS. ZOOKER

Yes.

TESH

And why?

MRS. ZOOKER

Well, I guess Mr. Rigley can answer that question better than me.

RIGLEY

Well, I think Mr. Tesh understands that church people do not usually associate the two institutions.

TESH

But, I think they *should* be associated, Mr. Rigley.

RIGLEY

Well —

TESH

Personally, I've always regarded them as simply different branches of the same profession. (*Rigley makes a sound of amusement, but Tesh cuts it off by a quick gesture*) Of course — I speak of the two institutions in their best sense.

RIGLEY

I'm afraid one doesn't see much of the best sense of the theater nowadays, Mr. Tesh.

TESH

One doesn't see anything at all, Mr. Rigley, if one doesn't look.

RIGLEY

That's true enough; but, then, one *hears* so many dreadful things of the people of the theater.

TESH

Perhaps, you mean one *reads* so many dreadful things.

RIGLEY

Well, probably, probably.

TESH

Frankly — I've read a great many very *shocking* things about church people (*Mrs. Zooker looks at Rigley*), but I

go to church occasionally; and I know some *very* good
people who go to the theater regularly.

RIGLEY

No doubt indeed.

LENA

I know some girl's got a ticket to see you to-night.

TESH

I'll leave a ticket for *you*, Lena, if you want to see me.

LENA (*suddenly seizing her mother's arm*)

Can I, Mom?

MRS. ZOOKER (*trying to silence her*)

Sh-sh-sh-

LENA

Can I?

[*Mrs. Zooker glances at Tesh with a shade of apology for
Lena's eagerness.*

MRS. ZOOKER

Well, you couldn't very well go alone, dear.

TESH

I shall leave a ticket for you, Mrs. Zooker; you can go
with her.

MRS. ZOOKER (*laughing a little*)

Well, I guess Mr. Rigley'd have to be consulted about
that.

TESH

I shall leave a ticket for Mr. Rigley, also.

[*They all laugh.*

RIGLEY

Thank you very much.

TESH

Bring him along with you — and, if he sees anything in
my play that in any way endangers your salvation —

why — then he need never allow you to go to the theater again.

RIGLEY

What is the name of your play, Mr. Tesh?

TESH

The Open Mind.

RIGLEY

The Open Mind?

TESH

The Open Mind.

RIGLEY

And what is the idea of it?

TESH

It's about a man who had an idea that he was very good; and that everybody else was very bad; until one night he went to see a play; and in one part of this play, the theater was so dark that the audience couldn't see one another. And, presently, he heard various people around him — weeping — over — the injustice that was being done to the hero, and later applauding, when the villain was killed; and it gave him an idea — That if people sitting in the dark — where nobody can see them — will weep — over injustice, and applaud the downfall of iniquity — why — these things must be very vital to them; — perhaps more so than they were to him, because he didn't weep; and he didn't applaud, either.

RIGLEY

What *did* he do?

TESH

He opened his mind, Mr. Rigley — wide open; because he saw that he had been mistaken all his life.

RIGLEY

And it took the theater to correct his mistake?

TESH

Precisely. The theater gave him the only opportunity that one has — of seeing people in the dark.

RIGLEY (*in a lighter vein*)

What did he *do* then, — become an actor?

TESH

No, no, — he became a minister. (*They all laugh. Mary passes up to the hall door and takes Tesh's hat off the hall-tree; then remains standing at the door*) So, you come along with Mrs. Zooker to-night, Mr. Rigley; you may get a very good idea for a sermon.

[*He turns away to the right, and goes to the hall door. Mrs. Zooker shoots across back of him and takes up her position just to the right of the door.*

RIGLEY

Indeed, that's very true, I might.

TESH (*turning at the door*)

And, Mrs. Zooker — (*He looks for her at the left of the door, and has a second's difficulty locating her*) I'll leave those tickets at the box-office for you. (*Mrs. Zooker smiles and nods*) That'll be, one for you — and (*He turns to Lena on the left of the door, and she indicates herself with an abrupt gesture*) Lena —

RIGLEY

And Mrs. Rigley and myself.

TESH

Just the four of you?

RIGLEY

Just the four of us, yes.

TESH (*withdraws his eyes slowly from him, then turns and extends his hand to Mrs. Zooker*)

Good-by, Mrs. Zooker.

MRS. ZOOKER (*shaking hands*)

Good-by, Mr. Tesh.

TESH

I'm very pleased to have met you.

MRS. ZOOKER

Thank you.

TESH

Although I'm sorry I couldn't have heard your daughter in one of her Irish numbers.

MRS. ZOOKER

Yes, it's too bad.

TESH

Well, some other time, I hope.

MRS. ZOOKER

I hope so too.

TESH (*turning to Lena*)

And, Lena — (*She thrusts her hand and arm towards him before he can extend his hand. He takes her hand and looks away off*) Lena — I think I shall see you some day — on Broadway.

[*She gives a sneering smile and slouches over to her mother, Tesh watching her with amusement.*

MRS. ZOOKER

Do you hear that, dear?

TESH (*turning to Rigley, who has come up at the left, and extending his hand*)

Mr. Rigley, I've had a very charming visit (*Rigley bows*), and I shall look for you to-night at the theater.

RIGLEY (*shaking hands*)

At the theater, yes; I'll call for those tickets at eight o'clock.

TESH

That'll be splendid. (*Turning to the door*) **Good** afternoon, Mrs. Zooker.

MRS. ZOOKER

Good afternoon, Mr. Tesh.

TESH (*nodding to Lena*)

Lena.

[*The curtain starts down very slowly.*

LENA

Good afternoon.

TESH (*glancing over his shoulder to Mr. Rigley, at the left of the door*)

Mr. Rigley, good afternoon.

RIGLEY (*bowing*)

Good afternoon, Mr. Tesh.

[*Tesh disappears into the hallway.*

TESH

I suppose my chauffeur is frozen to death. I'm going to send you my route from Chicago, Mary, and I'd like you to let me know occasionally what's happening to you —

[*Mrs. Zooker starts to follow Tesh out into the hallway, but Lena pushes her aside and rushes after him, much to the dismay of Mr. Rigley. Mrs. Zooker trails on out into the hallway after the rest of them, but Mr. Rigley remains standing just inside the hall door, to the left, looking intently at his resemblance to Edwin Booth in the photograph.*

THE CURTAIN IS DOWN

SMARTY'S PARTY

" — when Smarty gives a party — nobody ever
comes — but Smarty — not even his Mother."

(MRS. AUDENREID)

TO STEWART

"Smarty's Party" was first presented in New York City.

ORIGINAL CAST

MRS. AUDENREID	Rose Mary King
CHARLES	Harry Moore
MILDRED, his wife	Betty Barlow
MARIE, housemaid at Audenreid's . .	Mary Gildea

SCENE

The drawing-room of Mrs. Audenreid's apartment on Park Avenue, New York City, on a Saturday in late May, about four o'clock in the afternoon.

NOTE

The drawing-room is done in shades of orchid, with the draperies and piano scarf in blended silver-and-green brocaded satin. There's a black onyx bowl on the piano, filled with peach blossoms, and in the corner at the right there is an Italian marble pedestal with the statuette "Oiseau Libre" in solid gold. The floor rug is pale-green velvet, and the shades on the floor lamps on either side of the room are in the same tone — with black-and-silver tassels and trimmings.

SMARTY'S PARTY

The curtain rises, and all is still for a second. Then there is a sound of movement out at the left.

MRS. AUDENREID (*calling, out at the left*)

Oh, Marie!

MARIE (*out at the right*)

Yes?

[*Marie hurries in from the right and crosses towards the hallway at the left.*

MRS. AUDENREID

Will you take this, Marie.

MARIE

Oh, welcome home, Mrs. Audenreid!

[*She disappears into the hallway.*

MRS. AUDENREID

Hello, Marie.

MARIE

I'm certainly glad to see you back again!

MRS. AUDENREID

Will you take this, Marie.

MARIE

Isn't Charles with you?

MRS. AUDENREID

No, I must have missed him.

MARIE

Oh, isn't that too bad! (*The door closes*) I suppose you're tired, aren't you?

MRS. AUDENREID

Yes, I'm glad to get home.

MARIE (*entering, carrying a lady's satchel*)

That's always the way, isn't it? No matter where we go we're glad to get home again. (*She laughs faintly, and glances over her shoulder into the hallway. She's a womanly little person, in the regulation parlor-maid's black and white*) I guess I might as well take this right into your room, hadn't I, Mrs. Audenreid?

MRS. AUDENREID (*entering from the hallway, carrying an armload of pale-pink roses, a black silk French parasol, and a steel-colored, beaded hand-bag*)

Yes, if you will, Marie, please.

[*Marie goes out at the right with the satchel, and Mrs. Audenreid, tossing the hand-bag on to the table and the parasol on to the davenport, crosses over to the right to the piano and sets down the roses. She is a tall, thin woman, in her early forties — extremely aristocratic-looking, and wearing a very smart traveling-dress of dull green serge, with a full-length cape of the same material. Her gloves, slippers and stockings are all steel-colored, and she has on a small steel-and-green toque and a face veil.*

MARIE (*coming back into the room*)

Charles'll be terribly disappointed when he finds out that he's missed you.

[*She circles around and forward to the middle of the room.*

MRS. AUDENREID (*turning to her, from the piano, and commencing to remove her hat and veil*)

Are you sure he *went* to meet me, Marie?

MARIE

Well, he knew you were coming home this afternoon, for he told me so.

MRS. AUDENREID

Then, he got my wire all right?

MARIE

Oh, yes, ma'm; I gave it to him myself.

MRS. AUDENREID

Will you take this, Marie.

[*Marie takes the hat, and Mrs. Audenreid crosses to the window at the left, touching her hair.*

MARIE

That's how *I* knew you were coming home to-day. He told me. (*Mrs. Audenreid draws the window drapery aside and looks out — unfastening the collar-clasp of her cape with her disengaged hand*) There were four letters here for Charles besides the telegram. (*She finishes her settling of the hat and veil on the piano, and moves back again towards the center of the room*) I gave them all to him as soon as he came back.

[*Mrs. Audenreid turns sharply from the window and looks at her.*

MRS. AUDENREID

Came back from where?

MARIE

Ma'm?

MRS. AUDENREID

You say you gave him his mail as soon as he came back.

MARIE

Yes, ma'm.

MRS. AUDENREID

Had he been away somewhere?

MARIE

He was in Atlantic City.

[*There is a very slight pause, during which they look steadily at each other.*

MRS. AUDENREID

When?

MARIE

Why, he went away the day after you went away. And he was away from that till last Thursday. About ten days, I guess it must have been, altogether — that he was away.

MRS. AUDENREID (*removing her cape and tossing it on to the davenport*)

I suppose that's the reason I haven't heard from him.

[*She starts to take off her gloves, moving up to the end of the davenport and around to the head of the table.*

MARIE

Hasn't he written to you at all, Mrs. Audenreid?

MRS. AUDENREID

Not a line. (*She tosses the gloves on to the table, then reaches for her hand-bag and starts rummaging in it for her handkerchief*) That was really my principal reason for coming back so soon. I thought perhaps something had happened. I kept writing and writing, and getting no answers.

MARIE

Yes, I knew three of the letters that were here were from you, because I could tell your handwritin'.

MRS. AUDENREID

Was he ill or something — that he went to Atlantic City?

MARIE

I don't think so, Mrs. Audenreid; he didn't say nothing

to me. (*Mrs. Audenreid shifts her gaze, with a puzzled expression*) I guess maybe he thought it'd be too lonesome around here — with you away.

[*Mrs. Audenreid looks at her again.*

MRS. AUDENREID

Did he go alone?

MARIE

He left here alone. And he didn't say anything about anybody going with him.

MRS. AUDENREID

Did he say anything when he came back?

MARIE

No, ma'm, he didn't say much of anything. But he was awful sunburnt.

MRS. AUDENREID

It was Thursday my wire came, wasn't it?

MARIE

Yes, ma'm; the day before yesterday. It came about an hour before he came in. I don't know where he's been since then.

[*Mrs. Audenreid turns her head sharply and looks at her.*

MRS. AUDENREID

You mean he hasn't been here since he's been back?

MARIE

No, ma'm, I haven't seen him.

MRS. AUDENREID

Not at night, either?

MARIE

No, ma'm, — not that I know of.

MRS. AUDENREID

And he didn't say anything, when he was going out?

MARIE

Only that he'd be here this afternoon — when you'd get here.

[*Mrs. Audenreid shifts her eyes again, and thinks. Then she drops the hand-bag on to the table and starts around forward at the right of the table.*

MRS. AUDENREID

That's funny.

MARIE

That's why I thought he was at the dock to meet you this afternoon.

MRS. AUDENREID (*picking up several letters from the lower corner of the table*)

It may have been impossible for him to meet me. He may have had something to attend to. Are these letters for me, Marie?

MARIE

Yes, ma'm. I sent everything else right on to Bermuda. (*She turns to the roses and commences to settle them. Mrs. Audenreid opens one of the letters. Suddenly Marie turns again from the piano*) Oh, what about your trunk, Mrs. Audenreid?

MRS. AUDENREID (*reading the letter*)

Why, it'll probably be here sometime this afternoon, Marie, — or to-morrow morning. I left the check with the transfer people at the dock.

MARIE

Oh, did I tell you, Mrs. Audenreid, that Joe was workin' in the baggage room at the Pennsylvania depot now?

MRS. AUDENREID (*still reading, and abstractedly*)

Which Joe, Marie?

MARIE

Why, the young man that comes here to see me sometimes.

MRS. AUDENREID

Oh, yes, of course — I know Joe. And you say he's working at the Pennsylvania depot now?

MARIE

Yes, ma'm — on the outgoing baggage.

MRS. AUDENREID

And, does he like it?

MARIE

Yes, ma'm, he likes it very much. And then, of course, it's in the one place. And that's what he wanted mostly. He wants to be settled. Because every time he's ever said anything about getting married, I've always said I didn't see no sense to that, — if he was going to be away all the time. But he sez I have no excuse now.

[*She laughs a little.*

MRS. AUDENREID

Do you think you *will* marry him, Marie?

MARIE

Well, that's what I wanted to see *you* about, Mrs. Audenreid. I thought I'd wait till you'd get back, and see what *you* thought about it. I mean, you know, before I said anything.

MRS. AUDENREID

Do you like him well enough to marry him?

MARIE

Well, I think I'm used to him, more than anything else.

MRS. AUDENREID

Has he any money saved up?

MARIE

Yes, ma'm — up to April the first he had fourteen hundred and thirty-two dollars, — countin' the interest. I put it in the bank for him.   He sends it to me every week.   But I thought if I *did* take him, I'd want to let you know in time, — so you could get some one in my place.

[*There is a sound out at the left, in the hallway.*

MRS. AUDENREID

Well, that's very nice of you, Marie.

[*Marie steps up to the back of the room and looks out into the hallway.*

MARIE

I guess this is Charles now.

[*Mrs. Audenreid moves across towards the piano.*

CHARLES (*out in the hallway*)

It's cooler inside than it is on the street.

MILDRED (*out in the hallway*)

Yes, it's nice in here, isn't it?

[*Mrs. Audenreid comes to a stop beside the piano, listening.*

CHARLES

I'll close it.

[*Mrs. Audenreid turns sharply and looks at Marie, but Marie is still peering out into the hallway.   The door is heard to close; then Marie turns quietly and meets Mrs. Audenreid's eyes.*

MARIE (*simply*)

There's a young lady with him.

[*She starts towards the right to go out, looking steadily at Mrs. Audenreid.*

CHARLES (*still in the hallway*)

Right in this way, Mildred.   (*Marie glances over her*

shoulder, towards the hallway, and then goes out at the right. Charles enters from the hallway, removes his straw hat and holds it up in greeting to Mrs. Audenreid) Well, welcome to our city!

MRS. AUDENREID *(extending her arm and hand towards him)* The prodigal has returned.

[He laughs and strides across the room towards her. He's quite a good-looking chap, about twenty-two years of age, with a lot of dark hair. A rather sturdy type, in a dark-blue, well-cut double-breasted coat, and a pair of gray trousers, with a white pin stripe. And black, low shoes.

CHARLES

Hello, Mother. *(He kisses her, and pats her on the shoulder)* Glad to see you back.

[Then he turns away and takes a step or two back towards the hallway and looks out.

MRS. AUDENREID

But, where have you been, Charles?

CHARLES *(calling out into the hallway)*

Come in, Mildred.

MRS. AUDENREID

Were you at the dock?

CHARLES *(turning back to her)*

Why, no, Mother, I wasn't — I didn't go down to the dock.

[Mildred appears, up at the left, and stands, just inside the door, looking steadily at Mrs. Audenreid.

MRS. AUDENREID

I thought perhaps I'd missed you.

CHARLES

Did you just get in?

MRS. AUDENREID

Not ten minutes ago. I waited around the dock there for nearly fifteen minutes, thinking you'd come — (*He laughs a little*) but when I didn't see anything of you, I thought perhaps something had happened.

[*Mildred moves forward at the left, taking the room in with an appraising eye, and stands at the lower corner of the table, resting her right hand upon it, and her left on her hip. She's a perfect flapper, this one, — from the earrings to the slippers; very sharp and self-assured; with a shade of boldness in her personality that all the dove-gray of her cape and dress cannot entirely obscure. She's crafty, too, by the looks of her — in a thin-lipped way — and, somehow or another, rather common, — in the personal quality. — An impression quite apart from the heavy make-up or the bare arms. For, of course, her dress is entirely sleeveless, and much too short, — scarcely covering her knees. But then, her stockings are gray silk, to match her gloves and hat, so the effect is probably a studied one. She's very thin, about the legs, a kind of all-night dancer type, and quite young; maybe twenty-one; although it's extremely difficult to be exact, the way her hat is set down over her eyes. It's a small hat, trimmed with a pinwheel in Nile-green velvet and a narrow band of the same-colored ribbon. And out from under it, on either side, she has pulled two tufts of hair, — so ruffed and burned that it's quite impossible to determine just which of its shades, if any, was the original one. But, whatever degree of indefiniteness may attach to the color of her hair, there certainly can be no question as to the greenness of the long earrings — or the slippers. And she has a green hand-bag, too; and a green necklace. And the girdle of her dress — a kind of braided arrangement of*

*ribbon, knotted at the left side and falling in a side-sash
effect, with bugled ends — in silver, is also green. She's
all dressed up, — to meet Charlie's Mother; and as she
stands leaning against the table, waiting to be presented,
there's a hint of challenge in her steady ease.*

CHARLES

No, I was *going* to go down to the dock, but then I
thought maybe it'd be better to meet you here first.
(*He looks at Mildred and breaks into a laugh; which she
reflects; then he turns again to Mrs. Audenreid*) I've
got a little surprise for you, Mother. I want you to
meet Mildred, — my wife.

[*Mrs. Audenreid stands very still, looking at him. He
takes a step or two towards the back, acknowledging Mildred, — who crosses towards Mrs. Audenreid, rather
leisurely, with her hand extended.*

MILDRED

I'm pleased to meet you, Mrs. Audenreid.

[*Mrs. Audenreid takes her hand, abstractedly, keeping
her eyes on Charles, who swings nonchalantly over to the
left, and down to the back of the chair beside the table, where
he stands twirling his hat. There's a dead pause. Mildred
steps back a little from Mrs. Audenreid, looking at her
blankly, then backs a step, towards the back, following Mrs.
Audenreid's eyes to Charles. He has turned at the chair,
and stands looking questioningly from one to the other.*

MRS. AUDENREID (*in a level tone*)

Did you say your *wife*, Charles?

CHARLES

Yes, Mother; we were married a couple of weeks ago —
while you were away.

[*She continues to look at him steadily. He turns and puts*

*his hat down on the table, at his left, and Mildred turns and
looks at Mrs. Audenreid.*

MILDRED (*casually*)

A week ago last Monday.

CHARLES (*turning the chair around towards Mildred*)

Here, sit down, Mildred. (*She saunters across; and
Charles, thrusting his hands into his trousers' pockets, swings
carelessly to the middle of the room, smiling and very cocky*)
We went down to Atlantic City, the Monday after *you* left.
[*Mildred sits down and settles herself, touching her hair and
hat.*

MRS. AUDENREID (*quietly*)

Were you married in Atlantic City?

CHARLES

Yes; Mildred's sister went down *with* us; and a friend
of mine from the office, — Billy Righter. It was a
friend of Billy's that married us. He's a Justice of the
Peace down there. (*She regards him stonily; and he
breaks into a little self-conscious laugh, and turns away to
the left, crossing above the table*) I thought I'd give you
a little surprise when you'd get back.

[*He continues on down at the left of the table to the extreme
left, where he stands, balancing on his toes, — his feet very
far apart.*

MRS. AUDENREID (*in the same even tone*)

Did you surprise yourself, too?

[*He turns his head and looks at her.*

CHARLES

How do you mean, Mother?

MRS. AUDENREID

I mean, did you know you were going to be married when
I left here, two weeks ago?

CHARLES

Yes, sure I knew — It's been all set for over a month.

MRS. AUDENREID

And how is it you said nothing at all to me about it?

CHARLES (*smiling broadly, and with an attempt at banter*)

I thought I'd give you a little surprise.

[*He breaks into a rather slow, irritating laugh, and, swinging towards the table, throws his right leg across the lower corner of it and sits down. Then he looks at Mrs. Audenreid and laughs again. And Mildred joins him, faintly, by way of encouragement. But Mrs. Audenreid stands like a statue, — her hands closed on her necklace of aquamarine. There is a slight pause.*

MRS. AUDENREID

And how did you know I'd *like* to be surprised that way?

CHARLES (*his laughter freezing a bit*)

I *didn't* know.

MRS. AUDENREID

You know, there are certain kinds of surprises that a woman *never* likes; and one of them is surprises in connection with the marriages of her children. And I don't suppose I'm any different in that respect from any other woman.

CHARLES (*with a suggestion of pout, and flicking an imaginary speck of dust from his right knee*)

I didn't think you'd mind.

MRS. AUDENREID

No, I don't think you did. In fact, I don't think *you* did the thinking in this matter at all. (*He darts a quick look at her, and she holds it steadily. And Mildred, sensing the implication, looks quickly at Charles*) But, it doesn't matter now whether I mind it or not, does it?

(*She turns away slowly, to the right; and Mildred takes
advantage of the circumstance to lean quickly towards
Charles with a furtive instruction; to which he responds
with a narrowing of his eyes and a nodding of his head,
— signifying his complete understanding and control of
the situation. Then Mildred leans back again in her
chair; and Mrs. Audenreid turns, resting her arm on the
piano, and addresses her directly*)   Did *you* surprise *your*
mother, too?

MILDRED and CHARLES (*speaking together*)

{ (*Mildred*)   You mean, didn't I tell her?

{ (*Charles*)   No, Mildred told her mother, didn't you?
(*She turns and looks at him*)   *You* told your mother?

MILDRED

Oh, sure.   (*Turning to Mrs. Audenreid*)   *My* mother's
known about it all along.

CHARLES

Mildred's sister was *with* us.

MRS. AUDENREID

And did your mother know that *I* didn't know about it?

MILDRED (*becoming slightly disconcerted under Mrs. Audenreid's eyes*)

Well, I'll tell you — at first —

CHARLES (*sliding off the corner of the table*)

Listen, Mother.   (*He moves across below the table, to
about the middle of the room*)   Really, — the only reason
we wanted to keep it a secret was on account of Mildred's people not being in a position to go to the expense of a big wedding; so we thought the best thing
to do would be to just try and keep it as private as
possible.

[*Mrs. Audenreid holds his eye, for a slight pause.*

MRS. AUDENREID

I can't see how telling your mother would have made it a public occasion. She told *her* mother.

CHARLES

Yes, — I know she did.

MRS. AUDENREID

Then, why was all the surprise reserved for me?

CHARLES

It wasn't all reserved for you, now, Mother. Nobody else knew it but Mildred's mother and sister; and the fellow that stood up with me.

MRS. AUDENREID

But, why couldn't *I* have known it, too?

CHARLES

Well, Gee, I'm trying to —

MRS. AUDENREID

I was closer to you than Mildred's mother or sister, — or the fellow that stood up with you, either.

CHARLES (*with a touch of impatience*)

I've already *told* you, Mother — we didn't want to run ourselves into a lot of expense. (*She keeps mercilessly still, looking right into his eyes*) I mean, you've got to draw the line *somewhere*. If you tell one person, why, then you've got to tell somebody else. And then *he* tells somebody else, and the first thing you know the thing isn't a secret at all.

[*He thrusts his hands into his trousers' pockets and lounges up towards the door at the right, where he glances out abstractedly; then turns and starts across the room at the back.*

MRS. AUDENREID (*definitely*)

There is no reason why marriages that are all right should *be* any secret at all.

[*He comes to a dead stop, just a little to the left of the middle
of the room, and looks at her over his right shoulder, with
an expression of narrow inquiry.   Mildred is looking at
her too.   There is a little pause.*

CHARLES

Well, don't you think *this* marriage is all right?

[*Mrs. Audenreid turns her head easily and looks at him.*

MRS. AUDENREID

I don't know, — whether it is or not.

[*He holds her eye for a second; then Mildred shifts her
look to Charles, breaking the scene.*

CHARLES (*continuing over to the left, and with a touch of
swagger in his manner*)

Well, nobody has to do any worrying about it, I'll tell
you that.

[*He reaches the French window, down at the extreme left,
and, drawing aside the drapery, stands looking out.*

MILDRED

My sister was *with* us, Mrs. Audenreid, — and Mr.
Righter.

MRS. AUDENREID

I am not interested in *who* was with you.   I'm simply
inquiring into the necessity of so much haste — and
secrecy in the matter.   (*He turns impatiently from the
window to answer her, but she continues, directing the re-
mainder of her speech to him*)   And *why* during *my* absence.

CHARLES

Well, we've been trying to *explain* the reason to you for
the last fifteen minutes; (*he scowls at her and moves up
towards the back of the room and across towards the right,
above the table*) but *you* act as though we weren't telling
you the truth.

MRS. AUDENREID

Because I don't think you *are* telling me the truth. (*He stops, just above the middle of the room, and looks darkly at her*) There was some other reason for all this suddenness and secrecy; and I think I know exactly what that reason was.

[*They stand looking at each other.*

MILDRED

Charles didn't *have* to marry me, Mrs. Audenreid, — if that's what you mean.

[*She turns away, very indignant.*

MRS. AUDENREID (*steadily*)

I don't know anything about that, young woman.

CHARLES

Well, we're telling you, aren't we?

MRS. AUDENREID

But you have already deceived me — I can't reasonably be expected to trust you again. I must be allowed to come to my own conclusions from now on — as far as you two are concerned. And I daresay my conclusions in this particular case will be very similar to those that the majority of people come to, — in the matter of secret marriages. (*She sweeps them both with a look*) So you both may as well begin to accustom yourselves to the suspicion.

[*She turns away slowly, withdrawing her eyes, and moves to the piano bench, at her right.*

CHARLES

I don't think that's a very nice thing to say to Mildred, Mother.

MRS. AUDENREID (*sitting down on the piano bench*)

Don't you?

CHARLES

No, I certainly do not.

[*Mildred bursts into tears; and he moves to her side and puts his hand on her shoulder.*

MRS. AUDENREID

And what do you think about Mildred's consideration of *my* feelings?

CHARLES

Mildred didn't have anything at all to do with this, now, Mother, I'm telling you.

MRS. AUDENREID

Except to persuade *you* not to tell your mother.

CHARLES (*in a flash of anger*)

She didn't do anything of the kind!

MRS. AUDENREID (*raising her left hand, in deprecation, and rising*)

Please, Charles.

[*She turns to her left and goes up beside the piano towards the door at the right.*

CHARLES

Did you, Mildred?

MRS. AUDENREID

Don't champion Mildred; she doesn't need it.

[*She glances through the door to assure herself that Marie is not within hearing distance.*

MILDRED

I only said — (*She stops and coughs*) I didn't want Charles to tell you because I thought you might not want him to have me.

[*She continues to cry. Mrs. Audenreid comes back slowly towards the center of the room, looking at her with a questioning narrowness.*

MRS. AUDENREID

Why not?

MILDRED

Because we haven't *got* anything. My father's only a bookkeeper at the Weightman Chemical Works, and my sister works in the same office that I do. And I thought if Charles told you, you might not want him to *marry* a girl that didn't have anything.

MRS. AUDENREID

He didn't have anything himself; (*He gives her a quick, hard glance*) why should I expect the girl he'd marry to have anything.

MILDRED

Well, *you* had it; and I thought if he told you, you'd very likely —

MRS. AUDENREID

Did he *want* to tell me?

MILDRED and CHARLES (*speaking together*)

⎰ (*Mildred*) I don't remember whether he did or not.
⎱ (*Charles, impatiently, and moving a little away from the back of Mildred's chair, towards Mrs. Audenreid*) I didn't care one way or another *who* knew it. But Mildred's mother said *she* thought the best thing to do would be to say nothing at all about it to *anybody*, — till it was all over. So that's what we did.

[*He turns away, to his right, and takes a couple of steps towards the back of the room, then stands, looking off into the hallway, at the left.*

MRS. AUDENREID

Say nothing at all about it till Mildred was married to a rich woman's son; and then it wouldn't matter whether the rich woman liked it or not — that was it, wasn't it?

CHARLES and MILDRED (*speaking together*)
{ (*Charles, turning sharply*)   What?
{ (*Mildred*)   No, it wasn't it, at all.

MRS. AUDENREID (*turning away, to the right*)

It's all very simple, my dear girl.

MILDRED

It wasn't *that* I was thinking about at all — I *liked* Charles.

MRS. AUDENREID

Women do not try to persuade men they like into deceiving their mothers.

MILDRED and CHARLES (*speaking together*)
{ (*Mildred*)   I didn't *try* to persuade him into deceiving his mother.
{ (*Charles*)   It wasn't a question of anybody trying to persuade me into doing *anything*.   Mildred's mother simply suggested that we keep the thing quiet.

MRS. AUDENREID

And that was all that was necessary.   Simply a suggestion from a woman who was a comparative stranger to you, and you were ready to exclude from consideration the woman who has been more to you than anybody else in the world.   The right stuff isn't in you, boy.

MILDRED

It wasn't his fault at all, Mrs. Audenreid, that you weren't told.   It really wasn't — He didn't have anything to do with it.   But I thought if you knew, you might try to stop it.

[*Mrs. Audenreid turns and looks at her.*

MRS. AUDENREID

How could I have stopped it?   You were both of age, weren't you?

MILDRED

Well, we thought with *your* money you'd get around it some way.

MRS. AUDENREID (*directly*)

And you and your mother weren't taking any chances. [*Mildred is disconcerted for a second, then suddenly bursts into tears again. Charles scowls at Mrs. Audenreid, then crosses to Mildred and pats her on the shoulder.*

CHARLES

Don't cry, Mildred. (*But she cries harder. And there is a pause. Then he turns to Mrs. Audenreid*) I certainly don't understand your *attitude* in this thing at all, Mother, I'll tell you that.

MRS. AUDENREID

And you probably never will.

CHARLES

No, I don't think I will.

MRS. AUDENREID

But you probably *will* understand some day, Charles, how much *respect* a woman has for a man that she's able to dictate to in an issue as important as his marriage.

MILDRED (*in a flash of temper, and stamping her foot*)

I didn't *try* to dictate to him about his marriage! [*Charles lays his hand on her shoulder.*

CHARLES

Don't talk, Mildred.

MILDRED

Well, — she's not goin' to tell a lie about *me*.

MRS. AUDENREID (*with a cold expression of amusement, and moving a little away from the piano, towards the middle of the room*)

I'm not reproaching you at all, young woman. You've

simply done what a million girls of your type have done before you; and what millions more will do again. — But, you mustn't expect *me* to come to your party. For, in my opinion, it's the kind of party that no self-respecting woman *ever* goes to; because it's always a Smarty that gives it. And, you know, when *Smarty* gives a party, nobody *ever* comes — but Smarty — not even his mother.

[*She turns away slowly.*

CHARLES

Well, if I'd thought you'd make all this talk about it, I certainly wouldn't have said anything about it at all.

[*He swaggers across towards the left, crossing above the table, and on down towards the window.*

MRS. AUDENREID

It would have been better if you hadn't.

CHARLES

Well, I'm sorry now I did.

MILDRED

We never knew my *brother* was married till nearly a year and a half afterwards; and *my* mother didn't mind. *She* sez it only saves a lot of talk.

CHARLES

I'll say it does. — I'm sure *I* don't see what's so terrible about it. — Enough people *do* it.

[*He stops above the table, and picks up his hat.*

MRS. AUDENREID

I *read* about a good many of those people — in the newspapers.

CHARLES

I think a fellow ought to be allowed to keep *something* to himself.

MRS. AUDENREID

You'll be allowed to keep *this* thing to yourself.

CHARLES

Well, I guess I can do *that*, too. I'll have to tend to my own affairs *sometime;* I might as well begin now as any other time.

MRS. AUDENREID

You've already begun.

[*He senses the threat in her voice, and looks over challengingly.*

CHARLES

All right — I'm willing.

[*He turns away again.*

MRS. AUDENREID

And since you are to *have* the exclusive management of your affairs from now on, I should like to show myself a very good steward, — and turn them over to you with as accurate an accounting as possible. So sit down for a minute.

[*She turns away slowly, towards the piano bench, at her right.*

CHARLES (*sharply*)

I don't feel like sitting down.

MRS. AUDENREID (*quietly*)

I'd rather you would — (*she sits down, rather slowly, on the piano bench*); I have something very important to say to *you*.

[*He looks over at her, with a kind of narrow glare.*

MILDRED (*glancing at him, rather casually, but with the manner and tone of one accustomed to giving orders*)

Sit down.

[*He shifts his eyes to her, and she holds them for the fraction of a second, dead. Then he breaks the pause, and lounges towards the lower corner of the table, throwing his right leg across it and sitting down.   Mildred withdraws her eyes, opens her hand-bag, and looks at herself, in the little inside mirror, touching her hair.   Then she closes the hand-bag again and settles back in her chair, looking at Mrs. Audenreid.   Charles looks straight out, excluding Mrs. Audenreid.*

MRS. AUDENREID (*holding one of the stones of her necklace, and looking at it closely*)

I want to tell you first, Charles, — that you are not my son at all.

[*There is a physical stillness; then Charles looks over at her.   And Mildred, who has been looking steadily at Mrs. Audenreid, looks suddenly at Charles; then back again to Mrs. Audenreid.*

MILDRED

What do you mean, — that you're disowning him?

MRS. AUDENREID

I mean exactly what I said; that he is not my son.   So I couldn't very well disown him, could I? — for he never was my son.

CHARLES (*in a low, quick voice*)

Whose son was I?

MRS. AUDENREID

I don't know — whose son you were — your mother never told me — and I never asked her.

MILDRED

Well, who *was* his mother, then, if you weren't?

MRS. AUDENREID

She was a maid — that I had, before I was married.   And she was unfortunate, — if you know what I mean.

[*There is a second's stillness; then Mildred looks quickly at Charles.*

CHARLES

I know what you mean. I know what she means. You mean that my mother wasn't married, — that's what you mean, isn't it?

MRS. AUDENREID (*with cold precision*)

Exactly — (*He slides quickly from the table, and stands resting one hand upon it, looking at her, threateningly*) That is exactly what I mean.

[*He holds her eye a shade longer, then looks at Mildred; then throws his head back with a sound of amused derision.*

CHARLES (*striding across and up towards the door at the right, his eyes blazing at Mrs. Audenreid*)

You must think I'm a *kid*, don't you? — to believe any stuff like that!

MILDRED

I don't believe it either, Charles.

CHARLES

Ho! Ho! That's funny!

MRS. AUDENREID

It's true.

[*He whirls, right above the table.*

CHARLES (*furiously*)

Well, I don't believe it!

MILDRED

Neither do I, Charles.

MRS. AUDENREID

It's easily proved.

[*He snatches up his hat from the table, in his agitation.*

CHARLES

Well, we'll prove it, you can gamble on that!

MILDRED

I should say we will.

MRS. AUDENREID

It isn't always wise to set about proving a thing of that kind —

CHARLES

Well, we'll prove it, whether it's wise or not!

MRS. AUDENREID

Especially when it's true!

CHARLES

Well, I don't believe it's true!

MRS. AUDENREID (*lifting her hand, to silence him*)

Sh-sh-sh-

CHARLES

And don't say that again!

MRS. AUDENREID (*casually*)

Don't let Marie hear you.

CHARLES (*tossing his hat back on to the table and striding across towards the right door, glaring at her*)

I don't care *who* hears me!

[*There is a slight pause.*

MILDRED

I think if there was any truth in what you're saying, Mrs. Audenreid, Charles'd have heard something about it long before this.

CHARLES

I should say I would.

MRS. AUDENREID

Who was there to tell him?

MILDRED

Oh, somebody *always* knows about *those* things.

CHARLES

I should say they do.   And they don't forget to tell **you** about them, either.

[*He stops at the head of the table, and, picking up his hat,
stands fuming and irresolute.*

MRS. AUDENREID

Well, the only persons who knew about *this* thing were
my mother and myself; and *we* forgot to tell any one
else. We were very kind to your mother — kinder
than she was to us; for when she wrote me, after *you*
were born, asking me to take her back, I persuaded my
mother to do so. So she came back; and brought *you*
with her. I was abroad at the time; and when I got
back, you were nearly a year old. I remember the first
time I saw you — You were on the side lawn of our
house, trying to walk. You'd wandered around from
the back; and I stood watching you from the porch.
But you fell so many times that I had to go out to you
finally and take you by the hand. And after that you
used to come around every day, and stand holding out
your hand for me to take you for a walk. And I used to
go and take you. Every day. So that really I taught
you to walk. (*She turns away, and has a second or two of
difficulty, but, by a definite mental and physical effort, gets
hold of herself*) I became attached to you, naturally;
you were always wandering into my room for something
— that the others wouldn't give you — So that when I
married, two years later, I took you and your mother
with me. You were about three years old then; and
you were a very funny little boy. And then, one day,
about a year after I had been married, your mother
disappeared — (*he looks over at her, darkly*) — just went
away — without telling me anything — very much as
you did in this. I don't know where she went. My
husband tried to find her for a long time, on account of

you; but she'd covered up her tracks very well. One of the other servants said she'd seen her reading a letter a day or two before; that may have had something to do with it, I don't know. But, *you* were left. My husband suggested putting you into a *home* of some kind; but you were a delicate little fellow, and — I kept you. And then one day you called *me* your mother; and I became sentimental. I had no child of my own, — and I rather regarded it as a *test* of what kind of a mother I should be. And I'm afraid I've been tried in the balances and found wanting; (*she shifts her eyes to him — a steady, rather mournful look*) for I've been a very *foolish* mother — as far as *you* were concerned.

[*Mildred looks at Charles; but he is looking straight ahead; so she looks back again to Mrs. Audenreid.*

MILDRED

Wasn't he ever adopted?

MRS. AUDENREID

No — he was not — fortunately; so you and your mother will be spared the trouble of looking up his rights under adoption.

CHARLES (*turning sharply, and addressing Mrs. Audenreid*)

How *was* it I wasn't ever adopted, if you were so fond of me?

MRS. AUDENREID

Because, as I've told you, I was sentimental about you. (*He turns away, with a movement of extreme impatience, and looks out the window*) And I rather *resented* the idea of any legalization of my relationship to you. That seems very funny to me, Charles, — as I see you now.

CHARLES

It seems very funny to *me*, too —

MRS. AUDENREID (*bitterly*)

Very funny.

CHARLES

That you'd keep a thing like *that* to yourself all *this* time, if there was anything *to* it.

MRS. AUDENREID

Because I wanted to keep it from *you*. I didn't want your attitude to me, as you grew older, to be colored with any sense of obligation. I wanted you to think you *were* my son; nobody else seemed to be interested in *whose* son you were.

CHARLES (*taking a few steps towards her*)

Well, I'll tell *you*, if there's anything to what *you're saying*, I think *you've* deceived *me* a whole lot more than *I've* deceived *you*. Don't *you*, Mildred?

MILDRED (*rising*)

I certainly do.

[*She moves across to the left, below the table, and turns round to her left, looking bitterly at Mrs. Audenreid, across the room.*

MRS. AUDENREID (*rising*)

But I've deceived *myself* — more than I've deceived any one else, — (*she moves slowly towards the center of the room*) in believing that you were *worth* all the luxury and the advantage that I've given you.

CHARLES (*whirling upon her abruptly, and speaking with intense bitterness*)

Well, I don't thank you for *telling* me! I can tell you that. And I don't believe a damned *word* of it, if you want to know. (*He starts away, but turns suddenly back again*) I think you're just sore because I didn't tell you I was going to be married. And I'm glad now I *didn't* tell you, for you never told me anything.

[*He snatches up his hat from the table.*

MILDRED

I don't know why you'd *tell* Charles a thing like this, now, Mrs. Audenreid, when you've kept it to yourself all *this* time.

MRS. AUDENREID (*with a devastating aloofness*)

It's my way of disowning him. I never thought I should be able to tell him what I've told him just now; but he has shown himself so utterly lacking in all the qualities that I admire, — that I find it peculiarly agreeable to be *able* to tell him — that he isn't a drop's blood to me.

[*She turns away, to the right, and moves slowly to the piano.*

CHARLES (*striding towards her*)

Well, there's one thing I want to tell *you*, and that is that I want to know what Mr. Audenreid left me in his will. You needn't laugh! I know he left me *something*, and I want to know what it is! And if *you* won't tell me, I can very soon find out for myself. (*He turns away, towards the head of the table; and, as he catches Mildred's eye, she nods approval of his remarks*) I can use it now.

MRS. AUDENREID

Who *told* you Mr. Audenreid left you anything in his will?

CHARLES

Never mind who told me — *I* know he *did*.

MRS. AUDENREID

Then, why don't you go to Mr. MacIntyre and have him read you a *copy* of the will?

CHARLES

Well, I can do *that*, too.

MRS. AUDENREID

I wouldn't waste any time, if I were you; Mr. Auden-reid left you nothing, of course.

CHARLES

I don't *believe* you.

MRS. AUDENREID

Why *should* he, leave *you* anything — you were nothing to *him*.

CHARLES

I wouldn't believe you on your *oath*, now! — after all this *rot* you've been handing out about my mother and father. But, I'll make you prove it, I'll tell you that! Every damned word of it! (*He starts for the hallway door, at the left*) Come on, Mildred. (*But Mildred remains standing perfectly still, looking daggers at Mrs. Audenreid. Charles turns again just before going out into the hallway and extends his arm and hand in a threatening, straight-from-the-shoulder gesture*) Nobody can get away with that kind of stuff in front of *my* wife! (*He disappears into the hallway*) I'll make them prove it! [*There is a pause; then the front door is heard to slam violently. Mildred moves up towards the hallway door. There is a touch of defiance in the swish of her body; and as she passes the davenport her impulse to destroy something vents itself upon an innocent satin cushion, which she slaps, quite viciously, on to the floor.*

MRS. AUDENREID (*crossing to the table*)

Where do you want your husband's things sent? [*She sits down on the chair before the table and reaches for a pen and card.*

MILDRED .

I don't know where he wants them sent. To *my* home, I guess, for the present.

MRS. AUDENREID

Will you give me the address, please?

MILDRED

Two-thirty-one Hansberry Street, Brooklyn.

MRS. AUDENREID

What name?

MILDRED

Why, his *own* name, of course; whose do you think?
[*She looks out into the hallway, very much annoyed at Mrs. Audenreid's stupidity.*

MRS. AUDENREID (*very quietly, and without looking up*)

But, I don't *know* his name. (*Mildred pins her with a quick, bitter look. Then Mrs. Audenreid raises her eyes and looks at her, steadily*) So I'd better send them to you. (*She drops her eyes to the card again*) What is *your* name?

MILDRED

Mildred Coleman.

MRS. AUDENREID

I'll have the maid collect them this afternoon.

MILDRED

I think you'll be sorry, Mrs. Audenreid, for what you *said* to Charles this afternoon. (*Mrs. Audenreid puts down the pen, taps a small bell on the table and rises, — going over and up towards the door at the right*) I don't think it was a very nice thing to *say* to a young man, if you was to ask me. I know how I'd feel if anybody was to say a thing like that to *me*.
[*Mrs. Audenreid stops at the right door, turns, and looks back at her.*

MRS. AUDENREID

Young woman, — when you have been better than a
mother to some one, for as many years as I have been
to your husband, and then he does to you what your
husband has done to me to-day, — you may know another kind of feeling — the kind they say Hell has no
fury like. (*Marie very quietly appears in the right door,
and stands looking at Mrs. Audenreid. After a very
slight pause Mrs. Audenreid turns and sees her*) This
young woman is going.

MARIE

Yes, ma'm.

[*Mrs. Audenreid goes out, at the right door.*

MILDRED (*calling after Mrs. Audenreid*)

Oh, *she* don't have to show me out! (*Then she leans
towards Marie with a spiteful expression*) You don't
have to show me out! (*Marie stops dead, and looks
at her in blank astonishment. Then Mildred flounces
out into the hallway*) Nobody has to show *me* out.
I know my way out, without anybody showin' it
to me.

[*There is a little pause, followed by a violent banging of the
outer door. Marie stands aghast, with her hand against
her cheek. Then, suddenly, she glances back over her
right shoulder towards the right door; then hurries over,
above the table, and down to the window, at the left, and
looks out, wonderingly. Mrs. Audenreid appears in the
right door, and stands, looking at her.*

MRS. AUDENREID

That is Charles' wife, Marie.

MARIE (*turning quickly from the window*)

Ma'm?

[*She comes over, below the table, towards the middle of the room.*

MRS. AUDENREID (*moving forward, beside the piano*)

That is Charles' wife.

MARIE (*incredulously*)

His *wife*, did you say, Mrs. Audenreid?

MRS. AUDENREID (*touching the roses*)

Yes; they were married while I was away.

MARIE

Oh, you don't mean it, Mrs. Audenreid? (*Mrs. Audenreid nods*) Really?

MRS. AUDENREID

Yes, really. They were married in Atlantic City.

MARIE

And didn't he say nothing to you about it?

MRS. AUDENREID (*turning to her with a wan smile*)

He said he wanted to surprise me.

MARIE

Oh, — isn't that lovely! (*She laughs; and Mrs. Audenreid turns away to the right, helplessly*) But, the *nerve* of him! — I'll bet you pretty nearly died when he told you, didn't you, Mrs. Audenreid?

MRS. AUDENREID

Yes, I did.

MARIE

I should think you would. She's awful pretty, though, isn't she?

MRS. AUDENREID (*sitting down on the piano bench, and with a touch of weariness in her manner*)

Rather pretty.

MARIE

And she's stylish, too; I was just watchin' her there

through the window, goin' along the street. Are they goin' to *live* here, Mrs. Audenreid?

MRS. AUDENREID

No, they are not, Marie — I think I shall close this place up for a while.

MARIE

Do you think you'll go traveling again, Mrs. Audenreid?

MRS. AUDENREID

No, I think I shall get married too — (*she looks at Marie, who tilts her head a bit and opens her mouth and eyes in astonishment*) to Mr. Severn.

MARIE

Do you, Mrs. Audenreid?

MRS. AUDENREID

I've been telling him for a long time that I should never marry while Charles was single; but I'm like *you* now, Marie — I have no excuse.

[*Marie laughs faintly, and with a touch of embarrassment; and Mrs. Audenreid tries to smile.*

MARIE

Do you think I ought to *take* Joe, Mrs. Audenreid? You were just goin' to tell me when Charles came in.

MRS. AUDENREID

I think so, Marie. He wants you; and he gives you his money — that's a very good sign.

MARIE

Yes, he always does that; I'll say that much for him.

MRS. AUDENREID

And if he should ever *stop* giving it to you, — I shall always be glad to have you come back with me.

MARIE

Well, that's very nice of you to say, Mrs. Audenreid,

I'm sure. (*She looks away, and then adds, with ever so slight a shade of calculation*) I'll *tell* him that. (*Then she looks at Mrs. Audenreid again*) I think sometimes it's just as well — to let a man know you can get along without him. (*Mrs. Audenreid inclines her head a trifle, and Marie turns away, to the left, and moves over to the table*) They're not apt to get so ignorant then.

MRS. AUDENREID

There's a card there on that table, Marie, with an address on it. I wish you'd get Charles' things together and send them there.

MARIE

Yes, ma'm.

MRS. AUDENREID

Send them care of the *name* that's written there.

MARIE

Mildred Coleman? (*Mrs. Audenreid inclines her head*) Two-thirty-one Hansberry Street, Brooklyn.

MRS. AUDENREID

That's right. You can put them into the big trunk in his room.

MARIE

Yes, ma'm. Do you want everything to go, Mrs. Audenreid?

MRS. AUDENREID

Everything, yes. And I'd like them to go as soon as possible.

MARIE (*starting towards the door up at the right*)

All right, Mrs. Audenreid, I'll get them together right away.

MRS. AUDENREID

Please. (*Marie reaches the door*) Oh, Marie —

MARIE

Yes, ma'm?

[*She comes back, and down to Mrs. Audenreid's left, and stands. Mrs. Audenreid turns, quietly, and looks at her.*

MRS. AUDENREID

Marie, if you should decide to get married, — have you any idea *when* it would be?

MARIE

Why, any time at all'd suit *me*, Mrs. Audenreid — (*Mrs. Audenreid inclines her head slowly and looks away*) — just as long as I had time to let my *mother* know. (*There is a pause; and Mrs. Audenreid, who is sitting looking wistfully away off, suddenly contracts her brows into an expression of intense suffering and closes her eyes. Then she turns slowly and looks at Marie, — who has been regarding her steadily*) I'd want *her* to be here. Of course, it's a pretty long trip for her, all the way from Scranton; but, I don't know, I'm funny that way, Mrs. Audenreid; somehow or another, I wouldn't feel *right* about a thing like that unless my mother was here.

MRS. AUDENREID

All right, Marie, — whenever you're ready.

[*She withdraws her eyes slowly, and sits looking straight ahead.*

MARIE

Yes, ma'm.

[*She starts up towards the door at the right again.*

MRS. AUDENREID

I wish you'd put those roses in one of the other rooms.

MARIE

Yes, ma'm.

MRS. AUDENREID

They're taking the air in here. (*She drops her hands into her lap and sits looking at the backs of them. Then she looks straight out, steadily, from under her brows, and says in a level voice*)   The servant is greater than her lord.

THE CURTAIN COMMENCES TO DESCEND SLOWLY

MARIE (*turning suddenly and coming forward, with an inquiring expression*)

What'd you say, Mrs. Audenreid?

[*She stops at a point to Mrs. Audenreid's left, and stands looking at her, her arms full of the roses.*

MRS. AUDENREID (*without moving, and abstractedly*)

Nothing at all, Marie.

MARIE (*with an apologetic little smile*)

Oh, I thought you said something.

[*Mrs. Audenreid turns and looks at her, vaguely.*

MRS. AUDENREID

I was talking to myself.

MARIE

Oh, — (*She makes a faint sound of amusement, at her mistake*)   Excuse me.

[*Mrs. Audenreid tries to smile an acknowledgment of the apology, and Marie moves up towards the door, looking at the roses in her arms. Suddenly Mrs. Audenreid buries her face in her hands in a pang of bitter weeping. Marie senses the movement and turns and looks at her over the roses, — wonderingly.*

END OF THE PLAY

THE WEAK SPOT

" — everybody's superstitious — That's the
weak spot in all of us."

(JENNY)

The form of the present manuscript is exactly that in which this comedy was presented for two years in the principal Keith and Orpheum Theaters of the United States of America and the Dominion of Canada.

GEORGE KELLY

TO JAMES H.

"The Weak Spot" was originally presented in New York City.

ORIGINAL CAST

ARNOLD WEST . . . . Richard Ranier
MILLIE WEST, his wife . . . . . Della Evans
JENNY DRAKE, a peddler woman . Margaret Hoffman

SCENE

The dining room in West's house in a suburb of Philadelphia, on a Saturday afternoon in May.

THE WEAK SPOT

Mrs. West, a pleasant-looking woman of possibly thirty, in a blue gingham house dress and small white apron, is removing the fancy little table basket and centerpiece from the table. She is singing " The Love Nest." She crosses to the buffet at the right, sets down the basket and centerpiece, and picks up a folded tablecloth. A door out at the right is heard to close. Mrs. West, with a glance at the hall door, crosses back to the table and commences to spread the cloth. West comes in through the hall door at the back and comes forward taking a folded newspaper from his side pocket. He's an everyday type of man, about thirty-three, wearing a gray suit and a straw hat — a bit over one eye.

MRS. WEST

I thought you were going to the baseball.

WEST

It was raining in town at two o'clock, and I didn't think they'd play.

MRS. WEST

Didn't rain out here.

WEST (*standing down at the right, looking at the paper*)

I guess it didn't rain out there, either; I see here that they played all right.

MRS. WEST (*crossing to the buffet*)

The Giants win?

[*She gathers up the little fancy basket and the salt and pepper-shakers.*

WEST

Could any team win with that guy Douglas pitchin'? (*Mrs. West has resumed her singing of "The Love Nest" — in a disturbingly higher key*) All right, all right. [*He moves over towards the left of the center table.*

MRS. WEST (*turning to him sharply*)

Oh, shut up!

WEST

I will if you will.

MRS. WEST

Why don't you stop reading the baseball, then! Nobody's tryin' to stop you from doing that, are they?

WEST

I can *read*.

MRS. WEST (*bringing the basket and the salt and pepper-shakers to the table*)

Well, I can sing, too, if I like. And I won't ask your permission, either.

WEST (*sitting on the chair at the left of the table*)

Well, if you're doing it for me, you can let it go till the first of the month.

MRS. WEST (*wiping the silver top of the salt-shaker*)

Well, I'm not doing it for you, dearie; (*she drops the shaker; picks it up again, and secures the top*) nor anything else I can get out of; (*she gives the salt-shaker a dash over her left shoulder*) don't flatter yourself.

WEST (*starting suddenly, and pressing his hand to his right eye*)

What are you doing! What are you doing!

MRS. WEST (*turning to him in surprise*)

What?

WEST (*rising and moving to an armchair, which is further over to the left*)

What are you trying to do!

MRS. WEST

Did that go on you?

WEST

No, it only went in my eye. (*Mrs. West laughs and settles the things on the table*) I suppose you'd have the time of your life if you blinded somebody.

MRS. WEST

Oh, don't be such an old crab! I knocked the salt-shaker over.

WEST

You certainly must have given it some knock.

MRS. WEST (*resuming her arrangements*)

I don't mean I knocked it over there; I threw that over my shoulder.

[*He turns and looks at her.*

WEST

What do you mean, you threw it over your shoulder?

MRS. WEST (*stopping and looking at him*)

You never heard of anybody throwing salt over their shoulder?

WEST

Nobody but you.

MRS. WEST

Well, I wouldn't let anybody hear me say so if I were you; (*she starts over to the buffet*) they'll wonder where you were brought up.

WEST

I was brought up right here in this city, if anybody wants to know where I was brought up. And in a much classier neighborhood than the one you were brought up in.

MRS. WEST (*with a little shriek of derision, and coming back to the table with some cups and saucers*)

You'll never see that day, boy.

WEST (*resuming his paper*)

You know it.

MRS. WEST

Nor anybody belonging to you.

[*She sets the cups and saucers down and commences to wipe them with a little towel.*

WEST

Anybody hears about you going around the house throwing salt over your shoulder, they'll begin to understand what I've got to put up with.

MRS. WEST (*stopping in her work and looking at him steadily*)

Do you mean to tell me you didn't know that if you spill salt and don't throw a pinch of it over your shoulder it's bad luck?

WEST (*turning and looking at her compassionately*)

Say, it's a shame the way people kid you.

[*He turns away and reads his paper.*

MRS. WEST

Oh, is that so.

WEST

The next time we have chicken for dinner, save the wishbone, and I'll make a wish with you.

MRS. WEST (*settling the cups and saucers*)

I've got a fine chance of having much chicken for dinner while I'm married to you.

WEST

I guess I'd be all right if I could keep you running around from one dog show to the other.

MRS. WEST (*leaning over the table towards him*)

You'll never be all right, kid, while your head's the shape it is.

[*She crosses over to the buffet.*

WEST

You're only talking that way to discourage competitors.

MRS. WEST (*gathering up knives and forks at the buffet*)

Ha!

[*She drops one of the forks and picks it up again.*

WEST

Why don't you take a little vacation and give them a chance?

MRS. WEST (*wiping the fork that she dropped*)

Because I know what happened to you the last vacation I took.

WEST

I was here all right when you got back, wasn't I?

MRS. WEST

That's about all you were, though, boy. (*Crossing back to the table with the knives and forks*) I'd never have known it was you only for the signet ring. (*She drops the handful of knives and forks on to the table, causing him to start nervously. She glances at him, as she proceeds to arrange two places*) You'd better take off your hat — and stay a while.

WEST

What for?

MRS. WEST

Why, you don't want to be sitting there with your hat on when a lady comes, do you?

WEST

Who's coming?

MRS. WEST

I don't know who she is.

WEST .

What's she coming for?

MRS. WEST

I don't know any more about it than you do.

WEST (*becoming impatient*)

Well, how do you know she's coming here at all?

MRS. WEST (*straightening up, glaring at him, and indicating a point in front of the buffet with a definite gesture*)

Didn't you see me drop that fork there a minute ago? (*West pulls his hat down over his eyes, turns away, and slides away down in the armchair*) Oh, I guess there's nothing to that, neither.

WEST

I tremble for you if anything ever happens to me.

MRS. WEST

Well, let me tell you something, Arnold West — There's a whole lot smarter people than you believe those things.

WEST

A lot of poor fatimas like you.

JENNY (*out in the hallway at the right*)

Anybody home?

MRS. WEST

Yes? (*She steps to the hall door and looks out into the hallway*) Oh, hello, Jenny, is that you!

JENNY (*out at the right*)

Yes, back again, bag and baggage.

[*The front door closes.*

MRS. WEST (*coming a step or two back into the room towards her husband*)

Didn't I tell you a lady was coming. (*West removes his*

hat and tosses it back over his chair on to the couch at the back of the room. Jenny appears at the hall door) Come in, Jenny.

JENNY (*advancing at the right*)

I thought maybe you were busy, so I didn't bother ringing.

[*Jenny is a weird, poor creature, tall and spare; and quite old — probably sixty-five; with wisps of gray hair drawn tightly back, and wearing crooked silver spectacles. She is one of those almost mysterious figures that, on certain Saturdays, comes peddling notions to the women of the suburbs. Everything from camisoles to cough drops, Jenny has it — all in a battered-looking old black satchel, which she lugs from door to door — usually the back door. She is lugging this old satchel now, with both hands, as she comes into the room. And she looks tired — poor thing; she wanders far. But she seems cheerful. Jenny always seems cheerful; an impression that is probably heightened by a certain staccato positiveness of attack in speaking. Her clothes, aside from the obviousness of the fact that some one or another of her numerous customers has given them to her, always give the impression of having been thoroughly drenched by the rain, and then allowed to dry right on her back. As a matter of fact, that is precisely what happened to them to-day; for she was caught in quite a shower out in one of the northern suburbs of the city. But then, one drenching, more or less, could hardly help or hinder, to any appreciable extent, the general rattiness of Jenny's appearance; for everything on her looks as though it had weathered many gales. The hat, particularly, an old thing made of black satine, battered and rusty, and trimmed with a spreading rose in soiled white velvet, and the straggling remnants of a bronze-colored ostrich tip. And then there is the skirt — obviously made for a much larger woman — flapping and dipping recklessly about the muddy shoes — a veritable debacle in crêpe de chine. It is one of the old-fashioned skirts, with whole waves of goods in it; and Jenny is so flat and flanky that one finds himself, almost unconsciously, speculating as to just what arrangement she can possibly have come to at the waist line. A series of folds, most probably. However, the actual details are hidden by the flounce of an ancient mohair coat, tight-fitting and black, with leg-of-mutton sleeves and a fluted tail. This relic is removed a few minutes later, and then all is forgotten in the contemplation of another memory, perhaps even more venerable than the coat — a pink satin basque, with a high stiff collar; and trimmed with as many yards of buff-colored lace as it can boast years of life. Some very wealthy old lady must have given this to Jenny — And Jenny took it; without interest in either its intrinsic or historic value. She is not concerned with clothes; they are of the world. She takes them if they are given to her, asking no questions for vanity's sake; and if she have need of them, she wears them; and if not, — she passes them along to "the poor."*

MRS. WEST (*standing at the back of the table, resting her hand upon it*)

You're quite a stranger, Jenny.

JENNY

Yes, I haven't been around this way now for nearly six weeks. Guess it doesn't seem that long, though, does it? [*She laughs.*

MRS. WEST (*resuming her setting of the table*)

You look tired, Jenny.

JENNY (*inclining her head*)

Beg pardon?

MRS. WEST (*leaning towards her*)

I say, you look tired.

JENNY

Yes, I am a bit tired.

MRS. WEST

Sit down for a minute and rest yourself.

JENNY (*approaching the chair*)

Thanks, I will for a minute; but I can't stay; I'm behind my schedule now.

[*She sits at the right of the table, setting her satchel on the floor beside her — to the right.*

MRS. WEST

Yes, this *is* late for you, Jenny.

JENNY (*starting to remove her hat, which is secured by a strap of thin white elastic under her hair in the back*)

Well, I was caught in a shower out in Roxborough and had to stand under an awning for most an hour.

MRS. WEST

Did you get wet?

JENNY (*laughing a little*)

Yes, I got quite a shower bath.

MRS. WEST

That's too bad.

JENNY

I wouldn't have cared, only for my hat. (*She has it off by this time, and, holding it by the brim, tries to dash off any lingering drops of rain that may be still upon it*) I only got it last week. A woman out on Wayne Avenue gave it to me. She said it was a very good hat in its day. (*She holds it flat on her hand, and extends it towards Mrs. West for inspection*) Pretty, isn't it?

MRS. WEST

Yes, that's very nice, Jenny.

JENNY (*withdrawing it, and flicking it with her fingers*)

It's a western hat — She said her husband brought it to her from Dayton, Ohio, in 1912.

[*She puts it on again.*

MRS. WEST (*leaning towards her*)

Did you know you walked away without the coat the last time?

JENNY (*amused*)

Yes, I never thought about it till I got home.

MRS. WEST

I'd better get it right now or you'll go away again without it.

[*She starts towards the hall door.*

JENNY (*rising, and circling over towards the buffet*)

Do you like this coat, Mrs. West?

MRS. WEST (*stopping at the door, and coming back a step or two towards the table*)

Yes, that's very nice, Jenny.

JENNY

Pretty back, isn't it?

[*West looks over at her.*

MRS. WEST

Yes, that's fine.

JENNY

A woman out in Tioga gave me this. She said it was her mother's. (*Holding the coat open*) Pretty lining, wasn't it?

MRS. WEST

Lovely.

[*West looks from Jenny to his wife*

JENNY

They're very rich people. She says her daughter has eleven pairs of shoes.

[*Jenny emphasizes this bit of intelligence with a pointed gesture, and speaks as though it were an extraordinary circumstance.*

MRS. WEST

She's well supplied, isn't she?

JENNY (*laughing lightly*)

I should say so. (*With an instant transition to seriousness*) But they're very nice people. It was through them that my husband got into Jefferson Hospital.

MRS. WEST

How is your husband, Jenny?

JENNY

Why, he isn't coughing as much as he did, but he sneezes more.

MRS. WEST

This is *my* husband, Jenny, — I don't think you've ever met him.

[*West looks up from his paper.*

JENNY

No, I haven't. How do you do, Mr. West.

WEST

How do you do.

JENNY (*coming back to her chair, and speaking to Mrs. West*)

I thought that's who it was. (*Sitting down*) But he doesn't look a bit like you.

MRS. WEST (*laying her hand on Jenny's shoulder*)

I'm glad of that, Jenny!

[*She starts for the hall door.*

JENNY

Oh, ho, ho!

MRS. WEST and JENNY (*together*)

{ (*Mrs. West, going out the hall door*)   I'll get you that
coat, Jenny.

{ (*Jenny*)   Do you hear what she says, Mr. West?

WEST

I'm used to that, Jenny.

JENNY (*as her laughter trails away*)

I don't think she means it, though.   (*Looking suddenly at West*)   You don't look unlike *my* husband, Mr. West.

WEST (*looking up*)

Is that so?

JENNY

Especially since he's been sick.

WEST

What's the matter with your husband, Jenny?

JENNY

Why, nobody seems to know.   But I think myself he has chronic consumption.   (*West nods*)   The doctor down at Jefferson told me the only thing for me to do was to look on the bright side; so that's what I'm doing.

WEST

Well, that's a good side to look on.

JENNY

Well, that's what I thought.   So I go down there every Sunday night and sing to him.   I sing hymns.   I was always a great hand for singing hymns.   Of course, he says he'd rather hear something livelier, but then I think the hymns are better for him; because I think he's only waiting for the messenger.

MRS. WEST (*coming in from the hallway carrying a big coat made of tan Bolivia cloth and a neat little toque in gray panne velvet, trimmed with a green quill. She is talking as she comes through the hall door*)

Here's that coat, Jenny.

JENNY (*rising, and turning round towards the back of the room*)

Oh, thank you, Mrs. West.

MRS. WEST and JENNY (*together*)

{ (*Mrs. West, laying the toque on the table*) It'll be a little heavy for you right now, but it'll make a good winter coat.

{ (*Jenny*) I don't want to trouble you.

JENNY (*feeling the goods*)

Oh, yes, that's beautiful.

MRS. WEST

It's Bolivia cloth. (*Jenny looks at it nearsightedly*) I bought it two winters ago.

JENNY (*commencing to remove her own coat*)

I think I'll just try it on, Mrs. West, if you don't mind.

MRS. WEST and JENNY (*together*)

{ (*Mrs. West*) Yes, try it on.

{ (*Jenny*) See if it fits me.

[*She lays her own coat over the back of the chair at the right of the table.*

MRS. WEST (*helping her on with the coat*)

It'll be a little full for you in the body.

JENNY

Oh, that doesn't matter, Mrs. West.

MRS. WEST

But you can take it in a bit yourself.

JENNY (*crossing to the mirror in the buffet, and pulling the two sides of the coat forward*)

Feels nice and roomy.

MRS. WEST

You can just move the buttons over, Jenny; it'll be better.

JENNY (*looking at the coat in the mirror, at various angles*)

I don't know but I like it the way it is.

MRS. WEST (*picking up the toque from the table*)

And I brought this hat down, too, Jenny. (*Jenny turns from the mirror and comes towards Mrs. West*) It was my last winter's hat.

JENNY

Oh, that's a sweet little hat.

MRS. WEST

It's a very well-made hat.

JENNY

Panne velvet, isn't it?

MRS. WEST

Yes.

JENNY (*taking off her own hat and setting it down on the chair at the right of the table*)

I like a small hat.

[*She takes the toque from Mrs. West and puts it on backwards.*

MRS. WEST

Well, that's the first small hat I've ever had, and I don't seem to have been able to get used to it.

JENNY (*at the mirror*)

This is lovely, isn't it?

MRS. WEST

Turn it round, Jenny; that quill goes to the front.

JENNY (*turning the hat on her head*)

Oh, yes, I see now how it goes.

MRS. WEST

That's it.

JENNY (*turning suddenly to Mrs. West*)

That's right pretty, isn't it?

MRS. WEST

Bring it further down on your face, Jenny.

JENNY (*turning back to the mirror*)

I see.

MRS. WEST

Those small hats look better a little to the front.

JENNY (*turning back to Mrs. West with the hat over her right eye*)

Is that it?

MRS. WEST (*crossing to her*)

Not quite so much, Jenny. (*Settling the hat a bit farther up on Jenny's head*) Show a little of your forehead.

JENNY

Of course, it'll make all the difference in the world when my hair is fixed.

MRS. WEST (*stepping back from her*)

About that way.

[*Jenny turns to the mirror.*

JENNY

Say, I'll be right in style with this, won't I?

MRS. WEST

You can wear that when you go down to see your husband.

JENNY

That's right.   Only I'm afraid if he sees me in this, he'll think I've gotten into bad company.

[*She looks at herself again in the mirror.*

MRS. WEST (*laughing*)

He'll think he's married to a chicken.

JENNY (*turning to her sharply*)

What say?

MRS. WEST (*leaning towards her, and speaking with emphasis*)

I say, he'll think he's married to a chicken.

JENNY (*laughing, and turning to the mirror again*)

That's right, — he'll think I'm a chicken sure.   (*Coming towards Mrs. West, removing the coat*)   Well, these are certainly beautiful, Mrs. West; and I'm sure I'm ever so much obliged to you.

MRS. WEST

Well, now, I hope you'll wear them, and don't give them away; the way you did the shoes I gave you.

[*Jenny hands her the coat.*

JENNY (*removing the toque and placing it on the table*)

Well, of course, we must remember the poor.

[*She picks up her own hat from the chair.*

MRS. WEST (*folding the coat*)

Well, I guess you're as poor as anybody you'll give them to.

JENNY (*picking up her coat from the back of the chair and commencing to put it on*)

Yes, that's true enough, Mrs. West, I haven't much of this world's goods; but then, I have the understanding that my wants'll be provided; and we should be thankful for that, shouldn't we?   Don't you think we should, Mr. West?

WEST

Yes, that's right.

[Mrs. West steps to a little stand at the back of the room and procures a big piece of wrapping paper, which she brings to the table and spreads out. Then she places the folded tan coat upon it, and the toque on top of the coat, and commences to wrap them.

JENNY (*buttoning her coat*)

Only the other day I gave away my heavy coat to an Italian woman down at the mission; and there now, you're giving me another one; and a hat too. Now, ain't that beautiful! Ain't that beautiful, Mr. West?

WEST

Yes, that's very nice.

JENNY

You see, I took no thought for my body, wherewith I should be clothed; and there, you see, I am arrayed like a lily of the field. (*West makes a sharp sound with his paper, in shaking it out, which rather abruptly brings Jenny out of the momentary abstraction into which her quotation has induced her. She turns to her chair and sits down*) Do you think you'll need anything to-day, Mrs. West?

[She picks up her satchel, sets it on her lap, and opens it.

MRS. WEST (*busy wrapping the bundle*)

I don't know that I do, Jenny.

JENNY

Any tape for binding?

MRS. WEST

No.

JENNY

I have the biased tape, too.

MRS. WEST

I haven't used that that I got the last time yet, Jenny.

JENNY

Any rickrack?

MRS. WEST

No.

JENNY

You don't want any of that?

MRS. WEST

Um-um.

JENNY

Well, some one else'll want it. (*Taking a card of pale pink and pale blue garter-rubber out of the satchel, and handing it to Mrs. West*) Rubber for caps or garters? That's seven eighths of an inch wide. (*Mrs. West takes it, and puts it down on the table, and continues with her wrapping. Jenny returns to her rummaging in the satchel*) Pretty nearly an inch. Jewelry of all kinds? (*Taking a small finger-nail file out and holding it up towards Mrs. West*) There's a very nice finger-nail file, Mrs. West. Solid silver. (*Mrs. West takes it from her*) Fifteen cents. (*Mrs. West turns it over and looks at it*) You can use both sides of it. (*Returning to the satchel, while Mrs. West commences to file her nails*) Pins, plains and safety? Cough drops? Powder puffs? Hooks and eyes? Shoe laces? (*She draws out two shoe laces and holds them up*) Rights and lefts. These are the shorts, but I have them in the yard-and-a-quarter length, too.

MRS. WEST

I think I'll take this file, Jenny.

JENNY (*turning round to her and speaking with conviction*)

You'll go a long way, Mrs. West, before you get as good a bargain. Because that's just as good on one side as it is on the other. Let Mr. West see it. (*Mrs. West crosses to her husband, and Jenny returns to her satchel*) Oh, dear, what else have I here. Let's see. How about a nice little mustache comb for Mr. West?

WEST (*filing his nails*)

I haven't got any mustache, Jenny.

JENNY

Doesn't Mrs. West like them?

MRS. WEST (*standing slightly back of her husband's chair, resting her left hand upon it*)

I don't know whether I do or not, Jenny; he never had one.

JENNY (*turning back to her satchel*)

Well, he mustn't get discouraged. Beads? (*Draws out a rather long string of cheap-looking, red shiny beads, and holds them up towards Mrs. West*) I have them red and white. (*Mrs. West crosses over back of the table*) Ain't they beautiful? Real coral. (*Mrs. West takes them and examines them*) Ain't they beautiful, Mr. West?

WEST (*looking up*)

Yes, they're very nice.

[*Mrs. West goes over to the buffet mirror and adjusts them about her neck.*

JENNY

Those are twenty cents. You ought to buy a string of those for your wife, Mr. West, and keep it for her birthday.

WEST

She's run out of birthdays, Jenny.

JENNY (*laughing*)

Oh, do you hear what he says, Mrs. West?

MRS. WEST (*admiring herself in the beads*)

No, what'd he say, Jenny?

JENNY

I don't think I'd better tell you. (*Looking into her satchel again*) I never like to make trouble between man and wife. How about a nice breastpin, Mrs. West? (*She takes out a card with a queer-looking old brooch fastened on it, and extends it towards Mrs. West*) Diamonds and rubies. (*Mrs. West turns from the mirror and looks at it*) Ain't that beautiful? (*Mrs. West takes it from her*) Twenty-five cents. (*Returning to the satchel*) I have another here somewhere — set with diamonds and emeralds. No, I guess I must have sold it. But, here's a lovely tie-pin — Might interest *Mr.* West. (*She brings forth a weird horseshoe, made of highly colored beads; and holds it up towards Mrs. West*) Isn't that wonderful? Diamonds and sapphires. (*Mrs. West takes it from her*) That's twenty cents.

MRS. WEST (*looking at it*)

Yes, that's beautiful, Jenny.

JENNY

Let Mr. West see it. (*Mrs. West crosses over back of the table to West*) Those are real diamonds, Mr. West. (*He takes the pin from his wife and looks at it with a shade of amusement*) Twenty cents. I gave one of them to my husband last Christmas, and it looks just as good to-day as the day I gave it to him.

WEST (*handing it back to his wife*)

Yes, it's very nice.

JENNY

You don't think you care for it?

[*Mrs. West comes back towards the table with the tie-pin and the breast-pin.*

WEST

No, Jenny.

JENNY

Those are real diamonds.

WEST

Yes, you can see they are.

JENNY (*as Mrs. West hands the jewelry back to her*)

For my wholesale man told me so.   Don't want it, eh?

MRS. WEST

He wouldn't know what to do with diamonds if he had them, Jenny.

[*She continues over to the mirror.*

JENNY (*laughing*)

Oh, do you hear what she says, Mr. West!

MRS. WEST

But, I think I'll take these beads, Jenny.

JENNY

It's the mistake of a lifetime if you don't, Mrs. West.

MRS. WEST

Is this a good clasp, Jenny?

JENNY

That's as solid as the Rock of Garabaldi, dear.   And you won't get as becoming a bead again in a long time. And they're real coral too; (*turning her head to West*) for my wholesale man told me so.

MRS. WEST (*reaching up on to the little shelf of the buffet for some change*)

Twenty cents did you say these were, Jenny?

JENNY

Twenty cents, yes. I *have* gotten as high as twenty-five; (*turning to West*) but that was during the war.

[*Mrs. West steps over to Jenny's side.*

MRS. WEST

Here you are, Jenny — thirty-five cents.

JENNY

Thank you very much.

MRS. WEST (*holding Jenny's hand and placing the money into it*)

That's twenty for the beads, and fifteen for the file.

JENNY

That's right, Mrs. West. And thank you very much.

[*She takes a little old cash-purse from a pocket in the right side of her coat and puts the change into it.*

MRS. WEST (*stepping around back of the table and laying her hand, by way of indication, upon the bundle*)

And here's the coat and hat, when you're going. [*She moves across to the mirror again.*

JENNY

All right, Mrs. West, I won't forget them this time.

MRS. WEST

Did you have a good day to-day, Jenny?

JENNY (*commencing to replace the various articles in the satchel*)

Yes, I can't complain; I took in two dollars and sixty-two cents.

MRS. WEST

You must have gotten rid of quite a bit of stuff.

JENNY

Well, of course, a dollar of that was for telling fortunes.

[*She turns back quietly and settles something, deep in her satchel. West has turned his head and is looking at her; and Mrs. West is standing very still, looking into the mirror. There is a still pause. Then Mrs. West turns quietly, and, leaning against the buffet, looks seriously at Jenny.*

MRS. WEST

I didn't know you told fortunes, Jenny.

JENNY (*looking up suddenly*)

Oh, yes — I've told them all my life. (*Turning to West*) They come true, too. (*Turning back again to Mrs. West*) Didn't you ever have your fortune told?

MRS. WEST

No, I've often thought I'd like to go and have my fortune told some time, but he says I'm crazy.

JENNY (*turning towards West*)

Who, Mr. West?

MRS. WEST

Yes; he doesn't believe in those things.

JENNY

Well, people didn't believe the world was round one time, neither; but it was, just the same.

WEST

I'm not superstitious, Jenny.

JENNY (*knowingly*)

Oh, yes, you are, dear; everybody's superstitious — That's the weak spot (*she emphasizes the word by definitely touching the table with the forefinger of her left hand*) in all of us.

WEST (*shifting himself in the chair, into a more comfortable position*)

Well, it's not in me.

JENNY

Well, maybe you don't call it superstition; some people

don't. Some people call it hunches and intuitions; (*turning to Mrs. West*) but it's all the same thing. (*She looks straight ahead, and her eyes narrow into an expression of deep perception*) It's the wisdom of the soul, that's what it is. We all get flashes of it occasionally, but it's so hard to understand, that we say we don't believe it.

[*She sits shaking her head with a measured slowness. West and his wife are looking at her. After a second's pause, Mrs. West raises her eyes and looks at her husband. He taps the side of his head with his two fingers, and then flips his hand and turns away, to read*)

MRS. WEST (*crossing over slowly to the back of the table*)

How do you tell fortunes, Jenny?

JENNY

I run the cards. Do you want me to run them for you? I'll run them.

[*She reaches into a pocket in the lining of her coat and brings out an old deck of cards.*

MRS. WEST

Yes, but I don't want you to tell me anything bad.

[*She gathers up the bundle of old clothes from the table and takes it to the little stand at the back of the room.*

JENNY (*shuffling the cards*)

Well, of course, I must tell you what the cards say.

WEST (*turning a page of the newspaper*)

Tell her she's going to lose me, Jenny; that'll be something bad.

[*Jenny laughs.*

MRS. WEST (*returning to the table, and flipping her hand at him*)

No such luck.

JENNY (*laughing louder, and pointing a reproving finger at her*)

Oh, ho, ho! (*She sets the deck of cards on the table*) Will you cut those, dear.

MRS. WEST (*gingerly picking up half the cards*)

This way, Jenny?

[*West looks over.*

JENNY (*picking up the remaining half of the pack from the table*)

That's it. (*She runs the cards in her hands out into a straight row; then picks up the others, which Mrs. West has set down, and repeats the process. Then she rather solemnly clasps her hands together, presses them against her bosom, and leans forward — looking intently at the cards. Mrs. West very quietly moves around to the chair at the left of the table and draws it out to sit down. But, at this point, her husband, who has been watching the proceedings, catches her eye; and she stands still, looking at him — her hand on the back of the chair. He breaks into a half laugh; and, turning away, shakes his head from side to side as though deploring her credulity. But his derision is lost upon her. She simply withers him with a look; and sits down — falling into much the same attitude as Jenny. Then there is a slight pause. West reads his paper. Suddenly Jenny looks up at Mrs. West*) You're going to have three children, Mrs. West. (*Mrs. West doesn't move. West listens. Jenny looks back to the cards and then up at Mrs. West again*) Two boys and a girl. (*She looks sharply back to the cards again and then back to Mrs. West*) By your second husband.

[*West looks over at Jenny; but her eyes are back upon the cards.*

MRS. WEST (*leaning a little forward*)

Am I going to marry again, Jenny?

JENNY (*without looking up*)

That's what it says in the cards. (*Mrs. West turns her head sharply and looks at her husband — He resumes his paper*) There it is as plain as day.

[*Mrs. West turns back to Jenny.*

MRS. WEST

When is this going to be?

JENNY

It's in the sevens — Seven days, seven weeks, seven months or seven years. And you're going to have a very beautiful love affair, Mrs. West. (*West gives an abrupt little shout of derision, and goes right on reading. Mrs. West whirls round and glares at him*) With a dark gentleman. (*Mrs. West turns back again to Jenny*) Very beautiful. For there's a straight run of red cards to the ace of hearts. Very romantic.

MRS. WEST

Is this love affair to be with the man I'm going to marry? (*Jenny looks up at her*) My second husband?

JENNY

Yes; it's the same gentleman.

[*She returns to the cards.*

MRS. WEST

Do I know him now?

JENNY (*without looking up*)

Oh, yes; he's been in your life for a long time. (*Mrs. West rests her right elbow on the table and looks out, thoughtfully*) I see a spell of sickness. Very serious. It's in the blood line, but not very near you. It's a lady — middle-aged.

MRS. WEST (*abruptly coming out of her abstraction, and leaning towards Jenny*)

Does this man I'm going to marry live near here, Jenny?

JENNY (*without looking up*)

Within a mile.

MRS. WEST

Did I know him before I was married?

JENNY

You met him shortly after.

MRS. WEST

Do I see him often?

JENNY (*looking at her*)

He's avoiding you, dear, — on account of Mr. West.
[*She indicates West with a nod.*

MRS. WEST

But, you say I know him to talk to?

JENNY (*with her eyes on the cards*)

Oh, yes; you've often talked to him.
[*Mrs. West rests her elbow on the table again and looks out with an expression of intense concentration.*

MRS. WEST

I can't think who that could be.
[*West gives another little shout of derision; which is instantly answered by another glare from his wife.*

JENNY

He's quite dark. (*This turns Mrs. West back to Jenny*) There's some money coming to Mr. West. (*West looks out over his paper*) Quite a bit of money. (*He looks at Jenny, and his wife turns and looks at him*) It's in the tens.

WEST (*resuming his paper*)

Ten cents.

MRS. WEST

Oh, keep quiet! and don't be so smart.

[*She turns back to Jenny.*

JENNY (*looking up from the cards*)

What'd he say?

MRS. WEST

Nothing at all, Jenny; don't pay any attention to him.

JENNY

There's some bad news here for you, Mrs. West.

MRS. WEST (*becoming suddenly still, her hands resting on the edge of the table*)

Oh, don't tell me that, Jenny.

JENNY

Yes, here it is, dear, — plain as day — (*looking up at Mrs. West*) I'm sorry.

[*She looks back again to the cards.*

MRS. WEST (*without moving*)

Does it say what it is?

JENNY (*pushing her hat farther back upon her head, without taking her eyes off the cards*)

Wait a minute, dear, I'll get it for you.

WEST (*getting up and tossing his paper on to the chair*)

When am I going to *get* this money that's coming to me, Jenny?

MRS. WEST (*half-turning, and silencing him with a gesture*)

Keep quiet, she's thinking of something.

[*He saunters up back of his wife to a point above the table and stands watching Jenny's expression.*

JENNY (*looking up at him suddenly*)

What'd you say, Mr. West?

WEST

I say, when am I going to get this *money* that's coming
to me?

JENNY (*returning to the cards*)

Why, it doesn't look to me as though you were going to
get it at all, dear.

WEST

I thought you said it was *coming* to me?

JENNY (*looking up at him*)

So it is, dear; but you're not going to get it.
(*Mrs. West looks at him*)   Mrs. West is going to
get it.

[*Jenny indicates Mrs. West with a nod, and West looks at
his wife.   She makes a face at him.*

WEST (*very deliberately tapping the cards with his forefinger*)

Those are very wise cards, Jenny (*starting towards the
door at the left*) ; that's been going on around here for
the past five years.

[*He picks up his newspaper as he passes the chair.*

JENNY (*lost in the cards*)

Looks to me as though it might be insurance money.

[*He turns and looks at her.*

WEST

What was that, Jenny?

MRS. WEST (*turning to him sharply*)

Oh, go on about your business!   If you've got any to go
about.   (*He goes out at the left, and his wife turns back to
Jenny, very anxiously*)   Did you find out yet what that
bad news is, Jenny?

JENNY (*without looking up*)

Yes, here it is, dear. (*Looking up at her*)   But I'd
rather not tell you, if it's going to upset you.   (*There is*

a slight pause, during which they sit and look at each other steadily) It's about Mr. West.

[*Mrs. West sits very still. Then she looks out, with a shade of fright in her expression. Then she turns suddenly and looks out the door through which her husband has gone. Then she looks back at Jenny, who has been watching her narrowly.*

MRS. WEST (*rising, and with a kind of apprehensive slowness*)

Well, don't tell me what it is, Jenny.

[*She moves forward a step or two from her chair, holding the necklace of red beads with the fingers of both hands.*

JENNY (*still looking at her steadily, and after a slight pause*)

You don't want to hear it?

MRS. WEST (*instantly, and without moving*)

What is it?

JENNY (*after a glance towards the door at the left, to assure herself that West is not within hearing distance*)

You're going to hear of Mr. West's death. (*Mrs. West turns and looks at her blankly*) Heart trouble.

MRS. WEST (*speaking with quiet emphasis, and turning towards the back of the room*)

Now, I *told* you not to tell me anything bad, Jenny.

[*She continues up towards the couch, and then stands, looking out through the door at the left with a troubled expression.*

JENNY

Well, I must tell you what the cards say, dear. (*Indicating a certain card with her pointed finger*) There it is. There's the message. And there's the ace of spades. (*Mrs. West looks over her right shoulder at the cards. Jenny looks up at her*) Can't make anything else out of it. (*Mrs. West moves over nearer the door at the left, and*

Jenny resumes her study of the cards. There is a slight pause) But it's a funny thing, Mrs. West — I don't see any grief.

[*Mrs. West turns and looks at her.*

MRS. WEST (*moving back towards the table*)

You don't see any what?

JENNY (*still studying the cards*)

I don't see any grief. (*Looking up at her*) No sorrow.

MRS. WEST

Does it say when this is going to be?

JENNY (*definitely*)

Very soon. (*Mrs. West doesn't move*) It's in the run of the present. (*Mrs. West slowly straightens up, and looks out with a touch of frightened hopelessness*) Now, don't be troubled, dear; we've all got to go sometime.

MRS. WEST (*without moving*)

No, but I'm sorry you told me that, Jenny; I'll be worried now.

JENNY (*sweeping her cards together*)

No, if things are going to happen to us, it's better that we know it beforehand; then we can be prepared to meet them. (*Stacking the cards*) You don't want to hear any more?

MRS. WEST (*without moving*)

Not now, Jenny.

JENNY (*replacing her cards*)

Well then, I'll run along.

[*She rises.*

MRS. WEST (*still without moving*)

Don't forget the bundle.

JENNY (*picking up her satchel*)

No, I'll take that right along with me. (*She moves around towards the little stand at the back of the room, where the bundle is lying*) I won't forget it this time. (*She gathers it up with her left hand and starts for the hall door*) And I'm ever so much obliged to you, I'm sure. Good-by, Mrs. West.

[*But Mrs. West doesn't hear her. She is still standing looking straight ahead — lost in thought. So Jenny turns again, just before going out into the hallway, and looks back at her. There is a second's stillness. Then, suddenly, Mrs. West comes to herself, and starts towards Jenny.*

MRS. WEST

Good-by, Jenny.

JENNY (*coming back a step or two into the room and laying her hand on Mrs. West's arm*)

Now, let not thy heart be troubled, dear; he'll be better off. And you're a young woman yet. (*She leans back a bit and peers narrowly out through the door at the left; then shifts her voice into a key of confidence*) And he's only standing in the way of this other gentleman that the cards speak about. Good-by, dear. (*She vanishes into the hallway. Mrs. West moves slowly up to the hall door and looks out after her. When Jenny reaches the front door she calls back to Mrs. West*) Good-by, Mrs. West.

MRS. WEST (*listlessly*)

Good-by, Jenny.

[*The front door is heard to close; and then Mrs. West, with her right hand resting against the jamb of the door, turns and looks out — away out. Her eyes are troubled.*

WEST (*entering from the left, still carrying his newspaper*)

Did that *nut* go?

MRS. WEST

Yes, she's gone.

[*She turns slowly and looks at him.*

WEST (*sitting down in the armchair again*)

I suppose you know all about it now, don't you, — past, present, and future?

[*She continues to look at him, with a peculiar expression; then, still keeping her eyes upon him, she moves forward to the chair at the right of the table and rests her hands upon the back of it.*

MRS. WEST

Is there anything you want, Arnold?

[*He is reading the paper.*

WEST (*after a slight pause, and without looking up*)

What?

MRS. WEST (*withdrawing her eyes from him and looking away off*)

I say, is there anything you want?

WEST

I'd like to get something to eat, before it's too late.

MRS. WEST (*toying weakly with her beads*)

I mean, is there any certain *thing* you'd like?

WEST (*turning to her*)

Why? — Haven't you got anything in the house?

MRS. WEST (*haltingly*)

Yes; but I thought if there was anything *special* you'd care about, — I'd run out and get it. (*He resumes his paper; and, instantly, the meekness of his wife's tone strikes him. The absolute novelty of it. And its significance. He is startled into a furrowed stare, straight ahead;*

then he turns sharply and looks at her — She is looking tearfully at him. As their eyes meet, she breaks down and cries) Oh, Arnold!

[*She sinks into the chair at the right of the table, burying her face in her handkerchief. He straightens up and stares at her, in puzzled amazement.*

WEST

What's the matter? (*She cries harder. He jumps to his feet and crosses up back of the table*) What's the idea, Millie? what are you crying about? (*She's quite overcome. He has a second of intense perplexity; then it dawns on him. He straightens up and extends his arm and hand towards the hall door*) Did that *nut* tell you something? (*But Millie can only cry*) Well now, you start paying any attention to what the likes of her says, and she'll soon have you as cuckoo as herself! (*He has stepped up to the hall door and glances out into the hallway. Just as he does, Mrs. West has another outbreak of weeping. It brings him down on her right*) What'd she do; tell you something was going to happen to you?

MRS. WEST

No, she didn't.

WEST

Well, then, what are you bawling about?

MRS. WEST

She said something was going to happen to you.

WEST (*banteringly*)

What'd she say I was going to do, die?

MRS. WEST (*breaking out again*)

Yes.

[*He laughs uproariously, and crosses over to the left, in front of the table.*

WEST (*crossing*)

And you believed her!

MRS. WEST

She said she could see it in the cards, as plain as day!

WEST (*turning, and speaking over his left shoulder to her*)

Well, I certainly must say, Millie, you're a very intelligent woman.

MRS. WEST (*controlling her weeping, and speaking with conviction*)

Well, a fortune teller told Mrs. MacFarland, last Fourth of July, that her sister was going to die before Christmas; for I was with her when she told her. And on the tenth of October she died.

[*She commences to cry a little again.*

WEST (*with a gesture of dismissal*)

That's what you call mental telepathy — I read all about it in a magazine, a couple of months ago. It's like the wireless — You just flash what's in your mind, (*He illustrates the principle with a rather flashy flip of his right hand*), and somebody else gets it.

MRS. WEST

Well, it wasn't in Mrs. MacFarland's mind that her sister was going to die, when the fortune teller told her; for her sister wasn't even sick then. And she told her just how she was going to die and everything. And it came true, too.

WEST (*picking up the newspaper again*)

Well, you start believing that stuff, the first thing you know *you'll* be going around with a satchel selling diamonds for twenty cents.

[*He sits in the armchair and reads.*

MRS. WEST (*after a little pause, during which she dries her eyes*)

Well, do you feel all right?

[*He gives her a look.*

WEST (*turning back to his paper*)

Certainly I feel all right.

MRS. WEST

Well, you know your heart isn't any too good.

WEST

Oh, don't be silly!

MRS. WEST (*rising*)

Well, I can't help it, Arnold. (*She moves around to a point above the table, and then stands there — one hand resting on the table*) She looked so funny when she said that. [*There is a second's pause. She is looking straight out, away off. West quietly raises his eyes over the top of his paper and looks out — thoughtfully. Then he lowers the newspaper to his lap, and the expression of his eyes narrows. He turns and looks at his wife. But she is miles away. So he turns back and looks straight out again.*

WEST (*in a toneless voice*)

What'd she say?

[*Mrs. West looks at him, but doesn't seem to have the courage to tell him. He turns his head, suddenly, upon receiving no answer, and they look at each other.*

MRS. WEST

She said I was going to hear of your death. (*He bursts into laughter. And she bursts into tears; and starts for the kitchen door, at the right — above the buffet*) That she could see the message.

[*She goes out. And Mr. West is vastly amused — judging from his laughter. But gradually the laughter dies; and finally settles into a frozen, wide-eyed stare.*

WEST (*calling into the kitchen, with an attempt at nonchalance*)

When did she say this was going to be?

MRS. WEST (*coming out of the kitchen and straight over to the table, carrying a small plate of biscuits*)

What?

WEST (*in a more intimate tone*)

When did she say I was going to die?

MRS. WEST (*looking steadily at him*)

Why, she said right away. (*He holds her eye*) That it was in the run of the present.

WEST (*turning back to his paper, with a shade too much swagger*)

I ought to be getting ready, then, oughtn't I?

[*He makes a very vague sound of amusement.*

MRS. WEST (*setting down the plate of biscuits*)

Oh, I don't think it's anything to joke about, Arnold West. (*There is a violent ring at the front door. They both start nervously; then look at each other*) Oh, I'm as nervous as a cat! (*She goes up and out to the hall door to answer the bell. West sits still for a second, listening. Then he puts his right hand over his heart and listens for the beat. Then he rises and crosses over in front of the table to the buffet, where he examines his face in the buffet mirror, very critically. He is evidently reassured, and, turning away, gives himself several rather brisk little blows on the chest. He also delivers himself of a few little coughs, — very much as though an ability to cough were the evidence of perfect health. By this time he has reached the foot of the couch, and Mrs. West hurries in from the hallway with an open letter in her hand*) A boy just brought this — I can't make it out.

[*She hands it to him.*

WEST

What is it, a telegram?

MRS. WEST

No, he says it's from the Samaritan Hospital. (*She steps back to the hall door and glances out*) He says it requires an answer.

WEST (*glancing at the envelope*)

Who's it for?

MRS. WEST (*coming back towards him*)

He says he was just told to deliver it at this address. (*West reads it, and she stands watching him*) Can you make it out? (*West finishes reading it, raises his eyes and looks straight ahead, with a keen expression*) Do you know what it is?

WEST (*in a subdued tone*)

Yes, I think I know what it is.

[*He looks at it again.*

MRS. WEST (*on the verge of alarm*)

What?

[*He passes back of her hurriedly and goes out into the hall-way.*

WEST (*going through the hall door*)

Wait a minute. (*She stands listening to his voice at the front door*) All right, boy. Tell them I'll be out there inside of an hour. That's at Broad and Ontario, isn't it? — All right, I'll be right out there. (*The front door closes. There is a dead pause. Then West, holding the letter in his hand, appears in the hall door — and stands looking at his wife. His face is very serious. Mrs. West puts her hand to her bosom*) Can you beat that!

MRS. WEST (*a bit faintly*)

What?

WEST (*crossing over in front of her, towards the left*)

La Crosse must be dead.

[*He stops and reads the communication again.*

MRS. WEST (*following him with her eyes*)

Who?

WEST

Billy La Crosse. You remember him; he was out here one Sunday for dinner.

MRS. WEST (*taking a step or two towards him*)

That little fellow from Boston?

WEST

Yes, he's our agent up there.

MRS. WEST

Yes, I remember him. How do you know he's dead?

WEST (*turning to her*)

Why, he was in the city to-day; and he had to go out to the Aldine Trust on some business. And he borrowed my raincoat — And he didn't come back. And it says here (*he reads from the letter in his hand*), "Arnold West, 1725 Division Street, died in this hospital this afternoon at 2.43. Admitted at 12.05. Ambulance case. Heart collapse at 17th and Sansom — Advise."

[*He looks at his wife. She meets the look with a puzzled expression. Then she reaches her left arm towards him, till the fingers touch his sleeve.*

MRS. WEST

Arnold West?

WEST (*endeavoring to make it clear*)

He had my raincoat on. (*He passes down between the armchair and the table and continues over in front of the table towards the right. She moves slowly down after him, keeping her eyes on him*) And there were some letters of mine in the pocket.

MRS. WEST (*standing in front of the table*)

Was that your *good* raincoat?

WEST (*without turning*)

Yes.

MRS. WEST

Well, you'd better go right out there and get it; you know what they are in those hospitals.

WEST

I told the boy I'd be right out.

MRS. WEST

Do you want something to eat before you go?

WEST

Yes; sure.

MRS. WEST (*starting for the kitchen*)

It won't take a minute.

WEST (*sauntering back towards the front of the center table*)

Can you imagine that, though. And I never saw him looking better than he did to-day. (*He leans against the table*) Everybody was telling him how well he looked.

MRS. WEST (*from the kitchen*)

Is he married?

WEST

I don't think so.

[*She hurries in from the kitchen with a small towel in her hand.*

MRS. WEST

What are you going to do about it, Arnold, when you get out there?

[*She picks up a serving spoon from the buffet and starts to rub it with the towel.*

WEST

Tell them to notify McLaughlin; he knows where he lives in Boston.

[*He ponders the letter again.*

MRS. WEST (*standing over at his right*)

That's terrible, though, isn't it?

WEST

Pretty tough news for some one.   (*He sits very still; and Mrs. West gradually stops rubbing the serving spoon and looks away out, as though something had just occurred to her. Everything is still for a second; and then West becomes conscious of it; and, without moving, glances at his wife*)

What's the matter?

MRS. WEST (*with a suggestion of awe in her voice*)

That was awfully funny, though, wasn't it, Arnold?

WEST

What?

MRS. WEST

That that Jenny said, about hearing of your death.

WEST

Well, I'm not dead, am I?

[*She turns rather slowly and looks at him.*

MRS. WEST

She didn't say you were dead; she said we'd *hear* of your death.

WEST (*straightening up from his half-reclining position against the table*)

Well, you didn't hear of my death, did you?   It wasn't me that died.

MRS. WEST (*looking straight out again*)

I guess that's what she meant when she said she didn't see any grief.   (*He stops, his hand resting on the back of*

*the chair at the left of the table, and looks under his eyes at
her. She turns to him)* I suppose she meant — it
wouldn't be you that was dead, — but that we'd *hear*
it was you. (*He drops his eyes to the letter again; and
Mrs. West, keeping her eyes steadily upon him, moves over
to the chair at the right of the table and rests both her hands
upon it)* Arnold! (*He looks at her, sharply)* I wonder
how she knew we were going to *get* that message. (*He
draws the chair out and sits down, looking at the letter in
his hand. He abstractedly touches the salt-shaker, which
is at his hand)* And she said it'd be heart trouble, too.
(*He looks at her. She turns away with slow significance
and moves towards the kitchen. As he turns back to his
letter, he drops the salt-shaker on to the floor. Mrs. West
gives a start and turns; he sits frozenly still)* What was
that?

WEST (*looking at her with a taut indifference)*
Nothing.

MRS. WEST
I thought I heard something fall.

[*She goes out into the kitchen, he watching her till she is
out of sight. Then he darts a look at the salt-shaker on the
floor at his feet; and with a quick move, picks it up.
Holding it in his hands, he looks towards the kitchen.*

WEST
What did you say it meant if you spilt salt?

MRS. WEST (*coming in from the kitchen with a big spoon
in her hand; as though she had been stirring something)*
What did you say?

WEST
What did you say it means if you spill salt?

MRS. WEST (*halfway between the center table and the kitchen door*)

It means bad luck; unless you throw a pinch of it over your shoulder. (*He smiles with a weak derision, and turns away*) That's true.

[*She returns to the kitchen. He glances towards the kitchen, then looks at the spilt salt on the floor. Then at the letter in his hand, then at the salt-shaker in the other hand. Then, with another stealthy glance towards the kitchen, he flips some salt from the shaker over his left shoulder, sets the shaker down on the table guiltily, and turns away to reread the news of his death.*

THE CURTIN FALLS
RATHER SLOWLY

POOR AUBREY

A DOMESTIC COMEDY

" — it's silly to try to make an impression of any
kind; for the only one that'll be made'll be the
right one; and that'll make itself."

(MRS. FISHER)

The form of the present manuscript is exactly that in which this comedy was presented for two years in the principal Keith and Orpheum Theaters of the United States of America and the Dominion of Canada, and it was from its central character, Aubrey Piper, that the three-act comedy, "The Show-Off", was developed.

GEORGE KELLY

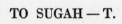

TO SUGAH — T.

"Poor Aubrey" was originally presented at the Palace Theater, New York City.

ORIGINAL CAST

AUBREY PIPER . . . . Frederick Sumner
AMY (his wife) . . . . Margaret O'Neill
MRS. FISHER (Amy's Mother) . . . Bertine Robinson
MRS. COLE (Marion Brill, — a friend
    of Amy's) . . . . Corinne Cantwell

SCENE

The sitting room in Fisher's house, about four o'clock of a Saturday afternoon in February.

POOR AUBREY

Amy enters briskly through the portières at the right, carry-ing a fancy cushion, which she sets in the armchair at the back of the room; then continues on over to an arched doorway at the left and draws the curtains together. She is a dark-haired, trim-looking woman, in her late twenties, dressed in black — a very pretty dress, of black crêpe, with a graceful side sash of the goods, piped with buff-colored silk. She has on black slippers and stockings, and wears a string of buff-colored beads — quite large. Her general manner suggests a quality of intelligent definiteness; something of which is even evident in the arrangement of her hair. While she is engaged at the curtains, the portières over at the right are brushed aside, and her husband swings into the room, and stands preening himself near the table. He is fearfully and wonderfully gotten up! — a perfect flash of cross-barred gray and brilliantine. Poor Aubrey! He is painfully arrayed, even to the toupee; a feature that, as Dickens remarked of Sairey Gamp's transformation, could scarcely be called false, it is so very innocent of anything approaching to deception. And the quantities of brilliantine that have obviously been employed upon it only serve to heighten its artificiality. He is wearing a glistening white vest and a shiny gold watch-chain, a necktie of living green, with a rather large horseshoe tie-pin of imitation diamonds, and a very high collar. He has a flashily bordered silk handkerchief set forth in the breast pocket of his coat, and there is a pair of heavy-rimmed nose-glasses depending from his neck on a black tape.

AUBREY (*touching his toupee gingerly*)

Does this thing look all right?

AMY

What?

AUBREY

This toupee.   (*She glances over her right shoulder indifferently*)   I put some of that brilliantine on it.

AMY (*resuming her arrangement of the curtains*)

It's all right.

AUBREY (*turning to the little wall mirror just below the portières at the right*)

You don't seem very enthusiastic about it.

AMY (*turning from the curtains and crossing quickly to the table — an oblong table, in the middle of the room, and towards the back*)

Because I don't think you need it.

[*She picks up a small folded cover from the table, shakes it out, and tosses it across her left shoulder; then commences to gather up the scattered books and put them into the little table-rack.*

AUBREY (*settling the toupee at the mirror*)

What do you want your friend to think, that you married an old man?

AMY

Why, a man doesn't look old simply because he hasn't a big head of hair.

AUBREY

Well, mine's pretty thin here on top.

AMY

Well, that's nothing; lots of young men haven't much.

AUBREY (*turning to her*)

Why, it was you that suggested my getting a toupee in the first place!

AMY (*stopping, and resting her hands on the table; and speaking directly to him*)

I know very well it was; because I knew I'd never have a minute's peace till you'd get one. All I heard morning, noon and night was something about your hair coming out. You might think nobody ever heard of anybody being baldheaded.

AUBREY (*turning back to the mirror*)

Well, a man's got to make the most of himself.

AMY

Well, if you think that thing's adding anything to *your* appearance, you've got another think. (*She starts towards the tabourette in front of the bay-window over at the left*) Lift up this plant here for me, I want to put this cover on. (*She picks up a dead leaf or two from the floor and tosses them out the window. He remains standing at the mirror, looking at the toupee very critically from various angles*) Aubrey!

AUBREY (*without moving, and with a touch of irritation*)

All right, all right!

AMY

Well, hurry up! — I want to change these covers. (*He withdraws lingeringly from the mirror*) You'll keep fooling with that wig till there isn't a hair left on it.

AUBREY (*crossing to her*)

It isn't a wig, now, Amy! I've told you that half a dozen times!

AMY (*raising her hand quietly, to silence him*)

Well, a toupee then, dearie, — don't get excited.

AUBREY

I'm not getting excited at all!

AMY (*indicating the plant with an authoritative gesture*)

Lift up this plant and shut up.   (*He lifts up the plant and holds it, till she has changed the covers*)   There.

[*He sets the plant down again, and she settles it more precisely.*

AUBREY (*starting back across the room, in front of the sofa*)

You just call it a wig because you know it makes me mad!

AMY (*straightening up and looking after him, with one hand on her hip*)

I don't know why it should make you so mad, to have it called a wig.

AUBREY (*turning to her sharply*)

Because it *isn't* a wig!   It's a toupee!

AMY (*turning to the plant again and giving it a final touch*)

Well, it's pretty, whatever it is.

AUBREY

It isn't even a toupee; it's just a patch!

AMY (*starting across to the back of the center table, carrying the soiled cover*)

It's a young *wig*, that's what it is.   (*He turns and glares at her.   She settles the scarf on the center table*)   And if it were only half as big as it is, anybody that'd look at it a mile away'd know that it never grew on you.

[*She goes quickly out through the portières at the right, and he returns to the mirror and preens himself generally. Immediately she comes back into the room again, carrying a big, dark dust-cloth, with which she commences to dust the center table; while he struts across the room in front of the*

*table, settling his cuffs and whistling the opening bars of
the chorus of "I'm Forever Blowing Bubbles."*

AUBREY (*as he approaches the bay-window*)

What do you say about putting a couple of these plants
out on the front porch?

AMY

What for?

AUBREY

I think it adds a lot to the appearance of the house as
you come up the street.

AMY

Oh, don't be silly, Aubrey!

AUBREY (*wheeling around and looking at her in astonishment*)

What do you mean, don't be silly?

AMY (*pausing in her dusting*)

Why, who ever heard of anybody putting plants on a
front porch in February!

AUBREY

I don't mean to leave them out there! We could bring
them in again as soon as she goes.

AMY (*starting for the little corner table down at the right*)

Yes, and she'd go away thinking we were both crazy.
*She arranges the few magazines on the table, and then com-
mences to dust it.*

AUBREY (*sauntering back to the center table, where he proceeds
to take the books which she has just arranged out of the
little rack, and stand them on their ends*)

Oh, everybody's thinking you're crazy, with you!

AMY (*turning to him and speaking emphatically*)

Well, I know that's exactly what *I'd* think, if I were to
come along and see plants on an open porch in the middle
of winter.

AUBREY (*occupied with the book arrangement, and without looking up*)

Well, I've seen *lots* of plants on front porches in the winter.

AMY (*returning to her work of dusting the table*)

Well, if you did, they were *enclosed* porches. (*She finishes the dusting, and starts back towards the center table; but comes to a dead stop upon seeing the arrangement of the books, and her husband's intense absorption in it. There is a slight pause*) What are you doing with those books?

AUBREY (*still busy*)

I'm just standing them up this way, so you can see what they are.

AMY

Can't you see what they are in the rack?

AUBREY

Certainly you can; but I think they show up better this way.

AMY (*stepping towards him and pushing him out of the way*)

Go away! and let them alone!

[*She hurriedly commences to gather them up and restore them to the rack.*

AUBREY (*wandering towards the arched doorway at the left*)

That's the way they have them in all the store windows.

[*He proceeds to push the curtains back at the arched doorway.*

AMY

Well, this isn't a store window. (*She glances at what he's doing, and starts towards him*) And don't push

those curtains back that way, Aubrey! I just fixed
them.

[*She pushes him towards the back of the room. He wanders
around her and comes forward at the left.*

AUBREY

They cover up the Victrola, that way.

AMY (*settling the curtains*)

That doesn't matter. These doors look too bare with
the curtains pushed back. (*She starts back towards the
center table to complete her rearrangement of the books*)
Now, let things alone, for heaven's sake! She can see
the Victrola when she goes in there.

AUBREY (*sauntering a little towards the right, in front of the
center table*)

She may not go in there.

AMY (*addressing him, as she crosses to the portières at the
right, taking the dust cloth with her*)

Well, I guess she's seen Victrolas before, even if she
doesn't go in there. (*She goes out through the portières.
He stands for a second fixing himself, then breaks into "I'm
Forever Blowing Bubbles" again. The detection of a
speck of dust on his left shoe brings his whistling to a close;
and, whipping out the eloquent handkerchief from his
breast pocket, he leans over to flick it off. The effort dis-
lodges the toupee, which drops to the floor in front of him.
He snatches it up frantically, and claps it back upon his
head; thrusts his handkerchief back into his pocket, and,
with a panic-stricken glance over his right shoulder, in the
direction of the portières, bolts to the bay-window, at the
left, holding the toupee in place with his left hand. Amy
hurries in from the right carrying a small vase, which she
takes to the little stand down at the right*) Any sign of her?

AUBREY (*adjusting the toupee, and pretending to look out the window*)

I don't see any sign of her yet.

AMY (*turning from the little stand and moving towards the front of the center table*)

Maybe her train's late.

[*She glances about the room, to see that everything is all right.*

AUBREY

I don't know why it *should* be; there wasn't any hold-up along the line to-day that *I* heard of.

AMY (*settling her sash*)

She said in her telegram that she'd get into Broad Street at three o'clock sharp, and that she'd come right out here — Because she had to leave again on the Bridge train at four-fourteen.

AUBREY (*turning from the window and coming towards her*)

Too bad she didn't know, she could have gotten right off here at North Philadelphia — And then she could have gotten that Bridge train right there again at — a — four-twenty-seven.

[*He finishes his remarks with an explanatory gesture, and stands looking at his wife. She is still settling her sash. There is a fractional pause. Then she finishes and looks up at him. Then there is another pause, during which her eyes shift to his toupee, which is on askew, — a bit over the left eye.*

AMY (*with a kind of wearied impatience*)

Fix your toupee.

AUBREY (*putting his hand to it, and with a note of challenge in his voice*)

What's the matter with it?

AMY

Why, it's all over the place.

AUBREY

Is that so!

AMY

Well, look at it!

AUBREY

Well, I fixed it that way!

[He emphasizes the remark with a little bob of his head, and starts up around the center table towards the mirror.

AMY

Well, it's pretty.

AUBREY

To let the air get to my scalp.

AMY

Well, for Heaven's sake, don't have it fixed that way when Marion comes!   (*Fixing the lace at her left cuff*) You look as though your head were lopsided.

[He turns from the mirror, and gives her a withering look. But she is occupied with her cuff.

AUBREY (*turning back to the mirror*)

How is it you didn't put on your other dress?

AMY

What other dress?

AUBREY

The one with all the beads.

AMY (*looking at him*)

Why, this is my good dress.

AUBREY

I think that other one's more of a flash.

AMY (*turning away again and settling the front of her dress*)

Oh, don't be such a show-off, Aubrey!

AUBREY (*turning sharply and looking at her*)

Show-off!

AMY

That's what I said.

AUBREY

I don't know how you figure *that's* showing off! — Because I want you to *look* good.

AMY (*looking at him stonily, and speaking in a level key*)

You want me to look good because I'm *your* wife. And you want this friend of mine to *see* me looking good; just as you want her to see that Victrola in there — (*she indicates the arched door on the left with a slight nod*) that isn't half paid for.

[*She looks out.*

AUBREY (*coming towards her a step or two*)

I suppose *you'd* rather have her think you married some poor thing!

AMY

Listen, Aubrey — It won't make the least bit of difference *what* we want her to think — She's a very smart girl; and all she'll have to do is glance around this room, and she'll know *exactly* what I married.

[*She looks straight out again.*

AUBREY (*mimicking her tone*)

Is that so! (*She simply emphasizes her remarks with a slow and very positive nod*) Well, now, you listen to me for a minute, Amy! You know I can beat it right over to the barber shop (*she breaks into a rather tired little laugh*) and stay there, till this friend of yours has gone, (*He moves over towards the little stand at the right*) if you're so awfully afraid that I'm going to show up so badly in front of her!

AMY (*looking after him with a very knowing expression*)

No fear of your beating it over to the barber shop.

AUBREY

No?

AMY

You'll be strutting around here in front of her if she stays till midnight.

AUBREY (*very nettled, and securing his tie and tie-pin*)

All right.

AMY (*taking a step or two towards him*)

And, by the way, Aubrey — When Marion comes — I want you to do me a little favor; and don't be giving her a lot of big talk, — the way you were doing to that insurance man the other night; (*he turns and looks at her in astonished indignation*) for I don't want her to think you're silly.

AUBREY

When was I doing any big talk to any insurance man?

AMY

The other night when you were talking to that man about the price of a fifty-thousand dollar policy.

AUBREY

Well, what about it?

AMY

Nothing; only that he was just laughing up his sleeve at you.

AUBREY

Is that so!

AMY

Well now, what else *could* he do, Aubrey? He knew you hadn't the slightest intention of taking any such policy.

AUBREY

How do you know he did?

AMY

Because he knows you're only a clerk. And that you don't get enough salary in six months to pay one year's premium on a policy like that. So when Marion comes, please don't be trying to impress her; (*she turns away from him rather slowly and moves up at the right of the center table*) for she's a very sensible woman.

AUBREY (*turning and going up to the mirror*)

I won't have anything to say to the woman at all.

AMY (*standing above the center table glancing through a magazine*)

Oh, yes, you will, dearie.

AUBREY

She's not coming to see me.

AMY

That doesn't make any difference to you.

AUBREY

No reason why I should stand around *gabbing* to her.

AMY

Well, you'll stand around gabbing, if you can get anybody to listen to you.

AUBREY

Well, now, you watch me.

AMY

I've been watching you; and listening to you too; for nearly four years.

AUBREY (*turning to her from the mirror, very peevishly, and holding up his right hand*)

All right, I'll raise my hand, — if I want to say anything. [*He moves forward at the right.*

AMY

I know what you'll do, if you get the chance; I've heard you before.

[*There is a slight pause, during which he frets a bit, down at the right. Then his mood shifts and he breaks into whistling his familiar "I'm Forever Blowing Bubbles." But this dies gradually as he becomes conscious of the little vase which Amy brought in for the stand at his right. He tilts his head a bit to one side and looks at it with critical disapproval.*

AUBREY

You know, it's too bad we haven't got something flashier for this stand here.

AMY (*just lifting her eyes over the top of the magazine*)

There's that vase up in mother's room.

AUBREY

Is she up there now?

AMY

She was when I came down.

AUBREY (*with a gesture of finality, and starting across in front of the center table*)

Well, *that's* out.

AMY

Why, she wouldn't mind my taking it.

AUBREY (*turning to his left and speaking emphatically*)

It isn't that! But if she sees you taking anything out of her room, she'll get an idea there's something going on down here, and she'll be right down for the rest of the night and you won't be able to chase her!

[*He turns to his right and looks out the bay-window.*

AMY

Why, she knows that Marion Brill is coming here this afternoon.

AUBREY (*turning to her sharply, with a distressed expression*)

Did you tell her?

AMY

Certainly I told her.

AUBREY (*despairingly, and crossing over again in front of the center table*)

Good night!

AMY

Why, I want her to *meet* Marion! She's never *met* her!

AUBREY

Well, if your mother ever gets *talking*, this friend of yours'll know everything from *your* age to *my* salary! (*He turns away to his right*) Now, I'm telling you!

AMY (*with a glance towards the portières at the right, and speaking in an emphatic but subdued manner*)

I don't care whether she does or not.

AUBREY

Well, I *do*.

[*Amy glances quickly towards the bay-window at the left; then, dropping the magazine, she steps eagerly towards it.*

AMY

There's a taxi, now.

[*She draws the curtain aside and looks keenly out.*

AUBREY (*whirling round and striding towards the bay-window, — holding on to his toupee with his left hand*)

Is it stopping?

AMY (*suddenly, and in a tone of suppressed excitement*)

There she is! (*She runs to the door at the back of the room and vanishes into the hallway)* She's looking for the number !

[*Aubrey peers eagerly through the bay-window, then steps quickly up to the door at the back.*

AUBREY

Don't stand out there talking, now, Amy, without something around you !

[*He rushes across at the back, still holding on to the toupee and, after a fleeting glance through the portières at the right, reaches the mirror, where he gives himself a hasty and critical survey. Then the laughter and greetings of his wife and Mrs. Cole reach him from the front door; so, with a glance in that direction, he struts forward at the right and strikes a pose, — swinging his nose-glasses carelessly back and forth, and looking away off.*

AMY *(out at the left)*

I knew you through the window of the taxi !

MRS. COLE]

Well, you know, I was thinking all the way out, "Now, I wonder if Amy got my wire."

AMY

I got it yesterday morning.

MRS. COLE and AMY *(together)*

{ *(Mrs. Cole)* Because, you know, I couldn't wait to hear from you.

{ *(Amy)* But I said to Aubrey, "There's no use in my sending any word now, for she's already left Chicago by this time."

[*The front door closes.*

MRS. COLE

Well, you see, dear, I didn't know *definitely* —

MRS. COLE and AMY (*together*)

    { (*Mrs. Cole*) Up until Thursday night that I was coming.
    { (*Amy, appearing in the hall door*) Oh, well, it
doesn't matter! (*Coming into the room*) Just so long as
I get to see you.

[*She glances at her husband, then turns and faces the hall
door. There is a second's pause; then Mrs. Cole enters
the room; and, glancing about, stops just inside the door.
She is a bit older than Amy, — probably three or four years,
and considerably lighter in coloring. And very smart.
Amy said she was, and she is — extremely so. It's in the
clearness of her eye, and the peculiarly deft coördination
of her general movement. Her clothes are smart too; and
by the looks of them, she must have married rather well;
they are quite gorgeous. A fine seal coat, full length, with
a cape effect, and an enormous muff made of black fox;
rather large hat of black lace over black satin, faced with
pale coral, and black slippers and stockings. She doesn't
remove her coat, but when she opens it, there is a glimpse of
a light coral-colored dress, heavily trimmed with steel beads,
a long neck-scarf in steel silk, and a lovely-looking necklace
of pale jade. She is wearing white kid gloves and carries a
fancy bag made of jade and coral beads on her left wrist.*

MRS. COLE

What an attractive house you have, Amy.

AMY (*smiling, and indicating her husband*)

There's the principal attraction, over there.

[*Aubrey acknowledges the compliment by melting slightly.*

MRS. COLE (*smiling graciously and passing down at the left
    of the center table, towards Aubrey*)

Is this *him?*

[*He advances.*

AMY (*coming forward at the left of the center table*)

That's him.

MRS. COLE

I'm *so* glad to meet you, Mr. Piper.

AUBREY (*with a touch of condescension*)

How do you do.

[*They shake hands.*

MRS. COLE

You know, I've always been enormously *curious* to see Amy's husband.

AUBREY

That so?

AMY (*looking straight out, and securing a hairpin in the right side of her head*)

There he is.

MRS. COLE (*tilting her head a bit to the left side and looking at Aubrey with a smile*)

He's terribly good-looking.

AMY (*turning away*)

Oh!

[*Mrs. Cole turns her head sharply and looks at her, still smiling.*

AUBREY (*addressing his wife*)

You hear *that?*

[*Mrs. Cole turns again to Aubrey.*

AMY

Please don't tell him that, Marion! he's bad enough as it is.

MRS. COLE

I don't know how you managed it, Amy. I could never do it. You should see *my* husband, Mr. Piper. I don't suppose he's any *older* than Mr. Piper, but, my dear, he *looks* old enough to be your father. (*Amy gives a little laugh of incredulity, and Mrs. Cole turns suddenly to her*) Really! (*Then she turns suddenly again to Aubrey*) He's almost bald!

[*Aubrey's smile freezes.*

AMY

Let me take your coat, Marion.

[*Aubrey turns quietly around to the right, touching his toupee with his right hand, and moves up to the mirror, where he takes a reassuring peep at it, unobserved.*

MRS. COLE

I don't think I'll bother, dear, really; that taxicab's waiting out there for me. You see, I've got to get that Bridge train out of Broad Street at four-fourteen.

AUBREY (*coming forward at the right*)

I was just saying to Amy, it's too bad you didn't know, you could have gotten right off here at North Philadelphia, and wouldn't have had to go downtown at all.

AMY

You know, that Bridge train makes a stop here, Marion, at North Philadelphia, on the way to Atlantic City.

MRS. COLE

Oh, does it!

AMY

Get's there at four-twenty-seven.

MRS. COLE

Isn't it too bad I didn't know that.

AUBREY

Well, you won't have to go back downtown now, as it is, will you, Mrs. Cole?

MRS. COLE

Yes, I've checked my grip at Broad Street.

AMY

Oh, isn't that too bad!

MRS. COLE

Well, it doesn't matter! Just so long as I got to see you.

AMY

That's about all you'll be able to do.

MRS. COLE

Well, sometime I'm going to invite myself to spend a few days with you, and then we'll have lots of time to talk.

AMY

I wish you could spend them now.

MRS. COLE

So do I, dear child; but what can a poor woman do with a sick husband on her hands.

AMY

How is he, Marion?

MRS. COLE

Why, he's pretty good, now.

AMY

Sit down.

[*She picks up the cushion from the right end of the sofa to make a place for Mrs. Cole.*

MRS. COLE (*stepping over to the sofa and unfastening her coat*)

I must unfasten this coat. (*Amy sits at the left end of the sofa; then Mrs. Cole sits down*) You know he had quite an attack of the flu last winter; and, I don't know, he never seemed to really get over it.

[*Aubrey has assumed a position over at the right of the center table, and is listening with a general expression of heavy consequence.*

AMY

So many people didn't.

AUBREY

One of the bookkeepers down at my office was telling me the other day that the flu has left him with a weak heart.

MRS. COLE

Yes, I've heard of that, too. But with my husband, it all seems to be in his nerves. That's the reason he's at Atlantic City now.

AMY

How long has he been there, Marion?

MRS. COLE

Since the week after New Year's.

AUBREY

They say Atlantic City's a great place for the nerves.

MRS. COLE

Well, Ralph says he feels ever so much better. I had a letter from him on Tuesday, and he said he was only going to stay another week. So I thought I'd better just run down there myself and see how he is before he starts that long trip back to Chicago.

AMY

That flu was a dreadful thing, wasn't it?

MRS. COLE

Dreadful! My dear, you've never seen anything change a person the way it has changed my husband. (*She turns suddenly to Aubrey*) He's even lost his hair. [*She coughs a little, and uses her handkerchief; while Aubrey glides to the mirror again, touching his toupee discreetly.*

AMY (*picking up the muff from Mrs. Cole's lap*)

I love this muff, Marion.

MRS. COLE

Do you know how long I've had that?

AMY

How long?

MRS. COLE

Three years last Christmas.

AMY

Really!

MRS. COLE

Ralph gave it to me the first Christmas we were married.

AMY (*holding it out on her left arm*)

It's beautiful!

[*Aubrey comes forward again.*

AUBREY

What kind of fur *is* that, Mrs. Cole?

MRS. COLE

Fox.

AUBREY

Makes a nice looking fur.

MRS. COLE (*turning and looking at it*)

It was pretty when I first got it. (*Turning again to Aubrey*) But it's getting old now; (*looking back to the muff*) the hair's commencing to fall out. (*He turns and drifts to the back of the room*) I was so sorry to hear about your father, Amy.

AMY

Yes, it was so sudden.

MRS. COLE

How is your mother, Amy?

[*Aubrey turns and looks towards his wife.*

AMY

She keeps pretty well.

MRS. COLE

That's good.

AMY

She's here with us, you know.

[*Aubrey makes a despairing gesture.*

MRS. COLE

Oh, is she?

AMY

Yes.

MRS. COLE

Living with you, you mean?

AMY (*getting up, and going round back of the sofa*)

Hum-hum.   I must tell her you're here.

MRS. COLE

Well, now, don't bother her, Amy, if she's doing anything.

AMY (*crossing to the portières at the right*)

Not a thing — She's crazy to see you.

MRS. COLE and AMY (*together*)

{ (*Mrs. Cole*)   I don't want to bother her.

{ (*Amy*)   I told her I'd call her as soon as you came.
(*Going out through the portières*)   I'll be down in a second.
[*Aubrey, standing up at the back of the room, glances after his wife, then turns and looks at Mrs. Cole. She is settling her muff beside her on the sofa. He glances at himself in the mirror, and then comes forward at the right, rather grandly, flipping the nose-glasses back and forth.*

MRS. COLE

Isn't it nice that Amy can have her mother here with her.

AUBREY

Yes; I've had her here ever since Mr. Fisher died.

MRS. COLE

She must be so much company for you.

AUBREY

Yes; a person'd never be lonesome.

MRS. COLE

I often say to *my* husband, I wish there were some one like that with us; I get so lonesome sometimes in the house during the day.

AUBREY

Well, when my father-in-law died, I thought Amy's mother might just as well come here with us. She was alone; and we had plenty of room; so I said, "Come ahead! (*He makes a rather magnificent gesture with his right hand*) The more the merrier!"

MRS. COLE

This *is* rather a large house, isn't it?

AUBREY

Yes, it is. Quite a wonderfully made house, too. They were put up by the McNeil people out here at Jenkintown. They're considered to build the best dwelling-house of anybody in the country. They just put up the twenty of them, as kind of sample houses — ten on that side, and ten on this. Of course, these on this side have the southern exposure; so a person's got to have quite a little pull to get hold of one of these. (*He catches his thumbs in the armholes of his vest, and, tilting his head a bit to the left side, looks away out and off, tapping his fingers on his chest*) But I have a friend — that's one of the biggest real estate men here in town, and he was able to fix it for me.

MRS. COLE

You were very lucky, weren't you?

AUBREY

Yes, I *was* pretty lucky in a way. Although I'd like to have gotten hold of one of the corner ones.

MRS. COLE

Are they a much larger house than these?

AUBREY

They're a fifteen-thousand-dollar house; these are only ten.

[*He moves across in front of her, with ever so slight a suggestion of strut.*

MRS. COLE

I see.

AUBREY (*with a casual glance out of the bay-window*)

I'm very anxious to get hold of one of them. I told this friend of mine to keep his eye open, and if there's a chance, I'll go as high as twenty thousand. Then, of course, I could always rent this.

MRS. COLE

It's an awfully nice street.

AUBREY

Nice in summer.

MRS. COLE

I was so surprised when I saw it, because the taxicab driver didn't know where it was when I asked him.

[*Aubrey looks at her, with a quick movement of his head.*

AUBREY

Didn't know where Cresson Street was?

MRS. COLE

He said not.

AUBREY (*shaking his head from side to side and smiling with heavy amusement*)

He must be an awful rube.

MRS. COLE

He had to ask the traffic officer down on Broad Street.

AUBREY

Well, I'll tell you — I don't suppose they *have* many calls for taxis out this way.   You see, most everybody in through here has his own car.

MRS. COLE

Oh, I see.

AUBREY

Some of them have a half a dozen, for that matter. (*He laughs consequentially, and she reflects his amusement faintly*)   I was saying to Amy, when we got your wire yesterday, it was too bad *my* car was laid up, I could have picked you up at the station to-day.

MRS. COLE

Oh, that didn't matter.

AUBREY

But I've been working it pretty hard lately, and I had to turn it in Thursday to have the valves ground.

MRS. COLE

There's always something to be done to them, isn't there?

AUBREY

I should say so.   Funny thing, too, — people have an idea if they get hold of a high-priced car their trouble's over.   (*She smiles and shakes her head from side to side in appreciation of that illusion*)   I swear, I've had just as much trouble with my *Pierce Arrow* as I ever had with my Buick.

[*They both laugh, and Aubrey looks out the window.*

AMY (*coming in through the portières at the right*)

Mother says she was just coming down to inquire how

it was you hadn't come. (*Aubrey turns and looks at his wife, then turns around to his right and moves towards the back of the room. Mrs. Fisher comes in through the portières, and Mrs. Cole rises*) This is Mrs. Cole, Mother — Marion Brill that you've heard so much about.

MRS. FISHER (*coming forward at the right of the center table*)

Well, indeed I have.

MRS. COLE (*advancing*)

I'm *so* glad to meet you, Mrs. Fisher.

MRS. FISHER (*shaking hands with her*)

How do you do. I'm certainly pleased to meet you, too.

MRS. COLE

Thank you.

MRS. FISHER

For I think I've heard your name more than any other girl's name I ever heard in this house.

MRS. COLE

Well, Amy and I worked beside each other so long.

MRS. FISHER

All I used to hear morning, noon and night was, "Marion Brill said so and so" (*Mrs. Cole and Amy laugh*) or, "Marion Brill is going to do so and so."

[*Mrs. Fisher laughs.*

AMY (*standing at her mother's right*)

I'm afraid that's about all we did was talk, wasn't it, Marion?

[*She laughs again.*

MRS. COLE

It's about all *I* used to do.

[*She laughs.*

MRS. FISHER (*indicating the sofa*)

Won't you sit down, Mrs. Cole?

MRS. COLE (*turning to her right, towards the sofa*)

Thanks.

AMY (*indicating the armchair at the right of the center table*)

Sit here, Mother.

MRS. FISHER (*passing to the armchair, in front of Amy*)

Amy, why didn't you ask Mrs. Cole to take off her coat?

MRS. COLE (*sitting on the sofa*)

She did, Mrs. Fisher.

[*Mrs. Fisher sits down.*

AMY (*sitting on the edge of the center table*)

Marion can't stay, Mother.

MRS. COLE

I've got to go almost immediately, Mrs. Fisher.

MRS. FISHER

It's too bad you can't stay for a cup of tea, anyway.

MRS. COLE

I'd love it, Mrs. Fisher, but I really haven't time.

MRS. FISHER

You're going to Atlantic City, aren't you?

MRS. COLE

Yes.

MRS. FISHER (*as though admitting a weakness in herself*)

I wish I was going with you.

[*She laughs shyly. And when she laughs she's pretty. She must have been a rather pretty girl; for there are traces of it yet; even after nearly thirty years as the wife of a poor man. Her husband was a wage-earner, always; and it was only by dint of vigilance and excessive scrimping that they were able to purchase and pay for the house in which she now lives. But the economic strain has told upon her, in many ways; perhaps, most obviously, in the*

*developing of a certain plainness of personal quality, —
a simplicity that is at once pathetic and, in a way, quaint.
And her manner of dressing and the arrangement of her
hair rather heighten this impression. She looks old-
fashioned. But her hair is quite lovely; it's thick and
silvery, with the loveliest wave in it; and she has it simply
parted in the middle and drawn back over her ears. She
must have been a decided blonde. Her dress, which looks
as though she might have made it herself, a long time ago,
has no particular pattern; simply a plain, brown poplin
dress, without a bit of trimming except a little ruffle of the
goods, about two inches deep, around the hem of the skirt.
This skirt is one of the old-fashioned, full kind, — touching
all the way round. She is wearing a deep lace collar,
probably to relieve the almost basque-like tightness of the
body, and an enormous breastpin, featuring a very vague
likeness of a delicate-looking gentleman in a straw hat;
presumably, Mr. Fisher.*

MRS. COLE

Do you like Atlantic City, Mrs. Fisher?

[*She nods, still smiling.*

AMY

Yes, mother's always been crazy about Atlantic City.

MRS. FISHER

I like the bathing.

MRS. COLE

Yes, wonderful, isn't it?

MRS. FISHER

I used to go in sometimes twice a day.

[*She laughs a little again.*

MRS. COLE

You must have liked it.

MRS. FISHER (*with an instant change to seriousness of expression and voice*)

Of course, that was before my operation.

[*Aubrey, who has been standing at the back of the room watching her with an expression of contemptuous pity, makes an impatient gesture and turns to the bay-window. Amy feels the movement, and, under the pretext of touching her hair, glances towards him.*

MRS. COLE

It certainly is a wonderful place.

MRS. FISHER

I haven't been there now since my husband died.

MRS. COLE

Is that so?

MRS. FISHER

Yes; it'll be four years the seventeenth of next October. He died the day Amy was twenty-five. (*Aubrey turns from the bay-window and looks daggers at her*) Died on her birthday. Didn't he, Amy?

AMY

Yes.

[*She glances towards Aubrey again, and he says voicelessly to her, but with very eloquent gestures, "Didn't I tell you!" and goes towards the back of the room again.*

MRS. COLE

And you haven't been to Atlantic City *since* then?

MRS. FISHER

No, not since then. But before that, we used to spend two days there every single summer. (*Aubrey turns at the back of the room and looks at her stonily*) Go down on Saturday morning, and come up Sunday night. Of course, it didn't cost us anything, you know, 'cept our fares; because we used to carry our lunch with us (*Aubrey begins to boil*) And in those days, they used to allow the excursionists to sleep under the board walk, if you remember.

[*Aubrey raises his hand in the hope of attracting her attention and silencing her; but she is oblivious of him. He's away up in the left-hand corner of the room, out of the range of Mrs. Cole's eye.*

MRS. COLE

Yes, I remember.

MRS. FISHER

Dear me, I used to look forward to those two days the whole year round. (*She laughs a little*) I was just saying to Amy the other day, that if I could see my way clear to do it, I believe I'd enjoy a day down there now, just as much as ever I did.

MRS. COLE

Well, I don't see why you shouldn't, Mrs. Fisher.

MRS. FISHER (*with another instantaneous shift to seriousness*) Well, of course, since my operation,

[*Aubrey makes a movement of excessive irritation, and Amy gets it; and thinks it wise to interrupt her mother.*

MRS. FISHER and AMY (*together*)

   (*Mrs. Fisher*) I've got to be more careful. I can't do the things — that — I —

   (*Amy, turning suddenly to Mrs. Cole*) *You* haven't been in Atlantic City since you were married, have you, Marion?

MRS. COLE

No, it's five years since I've been there.

MRS. FISHER

Are you going to stay there for any length of time, Mrs. Cole?

MRS. COLE

No, I'm not, Mrs. Fisher; I just want to see how my husband is.

MRS. FISHER

Has he consumption?

[*Aubrey snaps with irritation.*

MRS. COLE

No-o, he had the flu last winter; (*Mrs. Fisher folds her lips in, shakes her head slowly from side to side, and looks at the floor in front of her*) and he's never been exactly himself since.

MRS. FISHER

They never do much good after that flu.

[*Amy rises and crosses towards the left, above the sofa.*

AMY

I suppose it depends upon how bad a person's had it, Mother.

[*As soon as she passes out of the range of Mrs. Cole's vision, Aubrey appeals to her to know if there isn't something she can do to shut her mother up. She simply dismisses him with a deft gesture; and, with a sharp nod of her head, indicates the immediate presence of Mrs. Cole.*

MRS. FISHER (*unaware of the situation*)

Well, now, this doctor that tended me during my operation (*Aubrey whirls round and goes to the hall door, at the back, and Amy comes around and sits down on the sofa, to Mrs. Cole's left*) Doctor Stainthorpe — she's a lady doctor — she was telling me that the flu is like scarlet fever; if it don't leave you with one thing, it'll leave you with something else.

MRS. COLE

Well, Mr. Cole seems pretty good, most of the time, but

occasionally he has a spell of sort of — nervous exhaustion.

[*Aubrey wanders over and stands resting his right hand on the left end of the center table, listening to Mrs. Cole.*

MRS. FISHER

Maybe he works too hard.

MRS. COLE

No, I don't think it's that; (*speaking directly to Aubrey*) his work is easy enough. (*Shifting her eyes again to Mrs. Fisher*). He's just a wig-maker. (*Aubrey drifts towards the mirror*) Makes all kinds of hair goods, you know.

MRS. FISHER

Oh, yes.

AMY

I don't think I ever knew your husband's business, Marion.

MRS. COLE

Didn't I ever tell you?

AMY

You *may* have, but I've forgotten.

[*With a glance at his toupee in the mirror, Aubrey glides down at the right of Mrs. Fisher.*

MRS. COLE

That's what he does — Makes all these toupees that you see, — (*Aubrey turns quietly away to the right and glides up again towards the back of the room*) and switches and — patches — All that kind of thing.

MRS. FISHER

Did you have any trouble finding the house, Mrs. Cole?

MRS. COLE

No, not very much.

AMY

Marion came out in a taxi.

MRS. FISHER (*as though coming out in a taxi were quite an experience*)

Oh, *did* you!

MRS. COLE (*dropping her handkerchief at her left foot*)

Yes, I came right out Broad Street.

AMY (*handing her the handkerchief*)

Here's your handkerchief, Marion.

MRS. COLE and MRS. FISHER (*together*)

{ (*Mrs. Cole*)   Oh, thanks.   Did I drop that?
{ (*Mrs. Fisher*)   Have you any children, Mrs. Cole?

MRS. COLE

What did you say, Mrs. Fisher?

MRS. FISHER

I say, have you any children?

MRS. COLE

No, I haven't, Mrs. Fisher.

MRS. FISHER

Didn't you ever have any?

[*Aubrey looks helplessly at his wife, then back to his mother-in-law.*

MRS. COLE

No.

MRS. FISHER

Well, maybe you're just as well off.

MRS. COLE

Yes, I suppose I am, in a way.

MRS. FISHER (*looking at the floor in front of her, and shaking her head philosophically*)

If they never make you laugh, they'll never make you cry.

MRS. COLE

That's true.

MRS. FISHER

I buried a boy, when he was eight years old; and, dear me, it seemed as though I never in this *world* would get over it. But when I read in the newspapers now about all these bandits, and moving-picture people, — I'm kind of glad he went when he did. He might have gotten in with bad company and turned out just as bad as any of the others.

MRS. COLE

It's hard to tell how they'll turn out.

MRS. FISHER

Well, you see, this is such a terrible neighborhood in through here, to bring a boy *up* in. (*Aubrey makes a movement of controlled desperation towards the left. Amy glances at him, and he gives her a speaking look*) So many foreigners.

MRS. COLE

Is that so?

MRS. FISHER

Oh, it's just dreadful. (*Aubrey tries to signal her from the upper left-hand corner of the room, with divers shakes and waves of his hands. But it is utterly lost upon Mrs. Fisher. She is all set for a good chat; and it will require more than the gesticulations of Mr. Piper to distract her. So she goes serenely on; never even casting a glance in his direction*) A body'd be afraid to put their nose outside the door, after dark. Why, right across the street here (*she extends her arm and hand towards the right*) in two-twenty-eight, there's a big *Polish* family; and I don't believe there's a soul in that house speaks a word of

English. And there's a *colored* organization of some kind has just bought two-forty-nine — (*Aubrey has passed into a state of desperate unconsciousness, and stands glaring at his mother-in-law*) that's the corner property on this side. (*She points to the right*) Paid three thousand dollars cash for it, too. So you can see what the neighborhood's coming to.

AMY (*tactfully*)

Aubrey, — I wish you'd go down and close the heater; the house is getting cold again, I think.

[*He starts for the portières immediately, and Mrs. Cole turns and says something to Amy. As Aubrey crosses the back of the room, he fixes Mrs. Fisher with an icy glare, which he holds until he passes through the portières. Not knowing wherein she has offended, she turns and looks over her right shoulder after him with an expression of puzzled resentment. Then she turns to Amy.*

MRS. FISHER

Amy, you'd better go down, too; he'll be locking those grates again, the way he did last week.

AMY (*rising and going around back of the sofa and over towards the portières*)

He doesn't need to touch those grates; that fire's all right.

[*Goes out.*

MRS. FISHER

We have one of those old-fashioned heaters; and when you're raking it, unless you turn it just a certain way, the grates'll lock. It's a perfect nuisance. I often say, I don't wonder people want to live in apartments; where they won't have to be bothered with all this heater business.

MRS. COLE

It is a bother.

MRS. FISHER

Oh, it's a pest.

MRS. COLE

Although I had the hardest time getting used to an apartment when I was first married.

MRS. FISHER

Oh, do you live in an apartment in Chicago, Mrs. Cole?

MRS. COLE

Yes, I've lived in one ever since I've been out there.

MRS. FISHER

Well, you ought to be glad of it.

MRS. COLE

Well, really, it was the only place we could get — there have been so few houses go up in Chicago in the last few years.

MRS. FISHER

That's just the way it's been here. Why, when Amy was married four years ago, she couldn't get a house for love or money. That is, I mean, one that she could afford the rent, you know.

MRS. COLE

Yes, I know.

MRS. FISHER

Of course, she could have gotten plenty at fancy rents; but as I said to her, "How are you going to pay it on his wages?" (*She turns carefully in her chair and glances over her right shoulder towards the portières, for fear Aubrey might be within hearing distance. Then she turns back to Mrs. Cole, and, leaning towards her a bit, speaks in a rather subdued tone*) He's only a clerk, you know, — down here in the Pennsylvania Freight Office. But she couldn't get a thing. Of course, I'd have liked to have her stay here; because there was only Mr. Fisher and myself; but — a — (*she turns again and glances over her right shoulder, then back again to Mrs. Cole; this time with even more confidence*) my husband never liked *him*. (*She indicates Aubrey with a nod towards the portières. Then to emphasize the fact, she looks straight at Mrs. Cole and gives her head a little shake from side to side. But evidently she feels that she hasn't stated the circumstance sufficiently; or that, having mentioned it at all, it implies some measure of elucidation; for she rises gingerly, and, tiptoeing over to the center table, rests her left hand upon it and leans towards Mrs. Cole in an attitude of extreme caution and confidence*) Said he was kind of a blatherskite, you know — (*She tiptoes towards the portières, but stops halfway and turns again*) Very big ideas and very little brains. (*She continues on to the portières and glances out; then returns to the table*) So — a — finally, they had to take two little rooms over here on Lehigh Avenue. Nine dollars a month, so you can imagine what they were like. But you couldn't *tell* them anything. As I said to them, the night they first told me they were going to be married — I said, "How do you two ever expect to make ends meet on thirty-two dollars a week?" "Oh," he says, "that's only temporary," he says, — "I'll *own* the Pennsylvania Railroad within the next five years." This is the way he's owning it. (*She looks towards the portières; then turns back and says emphatically*) He's never even gotten a raise. He's been getting thirty-two dollars a week for the last four years. (*She moves stealthily towards the portières again; far enough over to enable her to glance through them; then comes back to the table*) But — a — as soon as Mr. *Fisher* died, I told Amy she could come here, and I'd take my rent out in board. And then she makes me different things to wear; she's very handy, you know.

MRS. COLE

Yes, she's a wonderful *girl*.

MRS. FISHER

But, you know, you'd think *he* was doing me a favor to *live* here. (*Mrs. Cole doesn't know exactly what to say, so she simply shakes her head from side to side and smiles*) He doesn't like me, you know. Hardly ever speaks to me. I suppose you noticed it, didn't you?

MRS. COLE

No, I didn't, Mrs. Fisher.

MRS. FISHER

He's been *furious* ever since last spring. (*She turns away again and glances towards the portières; then turns hurriedly back, as though she had a particularly incredible item of information to communicate*) Wanted *me* to put a *mortgage* on this house to get him an automobile. Can you imagine that! He's *crazy* about automobiles. And, Mrs. Cole, I know just as well as I'm standing here, that if he *got* one, he'd only kill himself — for he has no more brains than a rabbit. So I told him. I sez —

[*Amy's voice, out at the right, interrupts her.*

AMY

Be sure and close this cellar door Aubrey; there's a draught here if you don't.

MRS. FISHER (*tiptoeing back to her chair, with a significant gesture to Mrs. Cole*)

Well, I hope you find your husband all right, Mrs. Cole. [*She sits down.*

MRS. COLE

I hope so, thanks, Mrs. Fisher.   He *seems* pretty good, from his letters.

AMY (*coming through the portières*)

I'm sorry, Marion, but I seem to be the only one around here that knows how to tend to that heater.

MRS. COLE (*rising*)

Well, you know, you were always able to do everything, Amy.

[*She moves a little towards the front of the center table, fastening her glove.*

AMY

You don't have to go already, do you, Marion?

MRS. COLE

I'm afraid so, dear; (*Mrs. Fisher rises*) it's getting on to four o'clock.   (*Aubrey sways in through the portières, flicking imaginary ashes from himself with the fancy handkerchief.*

MRS. FISHER

Couldn't you take a later train, Mrs. Cole?

[*Aubrey comes forward at the right.*

MRS. COLE

Why, I suppose I could, Mrs. Fisher; but I've wired Mr. Cole that I'll be on *that* one.

MRS. FISHER

Oh, I see.

MRS. COLE

And he's so nervous and worrisome since he's been sick,

that I'm afraid if I'm *not* on it, he'll be tearing his hair
out. [*She turns, laughing a little, which Amy and her
mother reflect, and goes back to the sofa for her muff.
Aubrey is feigning a profound absorption in an examination of his finger nails. Amy crosses over after Mrs. Cole
and goes up back of the sofa towards the bay-window.*

MRS. FISHER

Are you going back to the station on the trolley, Mrs.
Cole?

MRS. COLE

No, I told the taxi to wait, Mrs. Fisher. I hope he's
still out there. Is he, Amy?

AMY (*at the window*)

Yes, he's still there.

MRS. FISHER (*hurrying across in front of Mrs. Cole*)

Oh, I must see it! Pardon me.

MRS. COLE

Certainly. (*Turning around to her right and going up
towards the hall door*) Now, Amy, I *do* hope you're
going to write to me occasionally.

AMY (*coming away from the window, towards her*)

You're the one who never writes.

MRS. COLE (*laughing guiltily*)

I know, darling; but I'm going to reform, really.

AMY

Well, now, I'm going to wait and see.

MRS. COLE

But, really, I've been so terribly busy since Mr. Cole's
been ill, that I don't seem to be able to —
[*She becomes confidential.*

MRS. FISHER (*turning, at the window, and addressing
Aubrey, who is standing directly opposite her at the right,*

and who happens to be the first one her eye lights upon)
Seems so funny to see an automobile in this street.
(Aubrey is paralyzed; and before he can recover the use of
his arm sufficiently to try to silence her, she has turned
again to the window; and he stands watching her, frozen
with the fear that she may turn again, and sustained only
by the hope that Mrs. Cole did not hear her. His agony is
very brief, however, for almost immediately, Mrs. Fisher
turns again and addresses him) I don't think I've ever
seen one in this street before. *(Aubrey makes a frantic*
gesture to her, and, turning around to his left, strides up
to the back of the room, pointing vigorously at Mrs. Cole.
Mrs. Fisher is bewildered — She simply stares blankly at
the goings-on of her son-in-law; and it is not until he
strides forward again at the right, glowering at her sav-
agely, that it occurs to her to speak) Why, what's the
matter with you!

[*Aubrey suddenly raises his left arm and hand as though*
he'd like to sweep her from the earth, but the opportune
turning of Mrs. Cole to say good-by to Mrs. Fisher,
restores order.

MRS. COLE

Good-by, Mrs. Fisher.

MRS. FISHER *(shaking hands with her)*

Good-by, Mrs. Cole.

MRS. COLE

I'm sorry to have to run away like this.

[*Amy moves around to Mrs. Cole's right.*

MRS. FISHER

Well, I know how you feel.

MRS. COLE *(turning and chucking Amy under the chin)*

But I *did* want to see my child here. And her husband

— probably the *best*-looking man I've seen in Philadelphia so far.

[*Amy, with an exclamation of deprecation, turns to her left and goes laughing out into the hallway. Mrs. Fisher laughs a little, out of courtesy.*

AUBREY (*swaggering up at the right of the center table, excessively self-satisfied, and pointing after his wife*)

Tell *her* that!

MRS. FISHER

I hope the next time you come this way you'll be able to stay a little longer, Mrs. Cole.

MRS. COLE

Thanks; I hope so, too, Mrs. Fisher. (*She turns to the right to greet Aubrey, who has come across above the center table*) Good-by, Mr. Piper.

AUBREY

Good-by, Mrs. Cole.

[*They shake hands.*

MRS. COLE (*dropping her glove at her right foot*)

I'm *so* glad to have met you. — Oh!

AUBREY (*stooping*)

I'll get it.

[*The toupee glides off and falls on to the black, fur rug on which they're standing; but he doesn't observe the circumstance, and restores the glove with a touch of flourish.*

MRS. COLE

Thanks.

[*She simply takes the glove, without the slightest evidence of an appreciation of the situation. But old Mrs. Fisher is in a state of siege; and, taking advantage of her position behind Mrs. Cole, endeavors to communicate to her son-in-*

law, by means of funny little pointings and movements with her head, some knowledge of his condition. But Aubrey is mercifully oblivious of everything, save that he is in the presence of a very attractive woman, who has admitted that she considers him probably the best-looking man she has seen in Philadelphia.

AUBREY

Sorry you have to go so soon.

MRS. COLE

I'm sorry, too, Mr. Piper. But if I'm not on that train, (*She turns to Mrs. Fisher*) I'm afraid I'll get scalped.

[*She goes out into the hallway.*

MRS. FISHER (*stepping to the hall door*)

Don't let her stand out there in the cold with nothing around her, Mrs. Cole.

MRS. COLE

No, I'll send her right in, Mrs. Fisher.

MRS. FISHER

Good-by.

MRS. COLE

Good-by.

AUBREY (*standing immediately behind Mrs. Fisher, looking out into the hallway*)

Good-by.

MRS. COLE

Amy, your mother says you mustn't stand out here in the cold with nothing around you.

[*Mrs. Fisher turns, and, with a glance at Aubrey, steps to the bay-window, to watch Mrs. Cole get into the taxi. Aubrey follows her and takes up his position just back of her, looking out.*

MRS. FISHER (*after a slight pause*)

Good-by. (*She waves to Mrs. Cole; and so does Aubrey, — perhaps with a trifle more dignity than the occasion implies. Then the taxi moves away, and they watch it, smiling, down the street. Suddenly Mrs. Fisher looks sharply in the opposite direction*) There's the boy with the paper. (*Turning from the window, folding her arms tightly together*) I've got to get my little woolen shawl (*she crosses to the right, above the center table*); this room's too chilly for me.

[*She goes out through the portières at the right. The front door, out at the left, closes; and Aubrey turns from the window to the hall door.*

AMY (*entering briskly through the hall door, carrying the evening paper*)

Here's the *Ledger.*

AUBREY

You ought to have something around you.

AMY (*stepping to the bay-window*)

I'm not cold. Where's Mother?

AUBREY (*opening the paper, as he strolls across above the center table*)

She's gone up for her shawl.

[*He sits in the armchair, down at the right, and Amy peers through the bay-window, as though trying to catch a last glimpse of the departing taxi.*

AMY (*suddenly turning from the window and coming across to the right, above the center table*)

Isn't Marion nice?

AUBREY

Yes, she's very pleasant.

AMY (*looking at herself in the mirror*)

She's an awfully smart girl, too. She had charge of our entire department when I worked at the Bank.

[*There is a slight pause.*

AUBREY (*half-turning, and very significantly*)

Say, Amy.

AMY

What?

AUBREY

Listen.

[*She turns her head sharply and looks at him. He beckons her to him with a rather mysterious nod, and she comes around to his left.*

AMY

What?

AUBREY (*in a subdued, level tone*)

Did you get your mother telling her your **age**?

AMY

That's nothing; Marion knows my age.

AUBREY

I *told* you what she'd do.

AMY (*starting towards the portières*)

Well, now, it doesn't make the least bit of **difference**; so don't start anything.

[*She glances through the portières.*

AUBREY

It's a good thing she didn't have any longer to stay.

MRS. FISHER (*out at the right*)

You know, Amy, —

AMY (*turning suddenly to him with a deft gesture*)

Sh — sh —

[*She steps to the mirror and pretends to be fixing her hair.*

AUBREY

Or she'd have told her a whole lot more.

MRS. FISHER (*coming through the portières wearing a rather skimpy-looking white shoulder-shawl and carrying some pale-pink knitting*)

I always pictured that girl as a much bigger woman than she is, when you used to talk about her.

[*She walks down between Aubrey and the center table and crosses over to the sofa. She appears to be having difficulty in disentangling her yarn.*

AMY

Don't you think she's a big girl?

MRS. FISHER

Well, *stouter*, I mean.

AMY

No, she never was stout.

MRS. FISHER (*sitting on the sofa, and settling herself*)

I'd never know her in the world from that picture you have of her upstairs.

AMY (*turning from the mirror*)

Don't you think she's nice?

MRS. FISHER

Very nice.

AMY (*standing at her husband's right*)

Give me a piece of that paper.

MRS. FISHER

And very stylish, too.

AMY

Any part'll do.

[*He detaches a section of the paper and gives it to her. She moves a step or two to the right and forward and commences to read. Aubrey resumes his reading; and Mrs. Fisher knits.*

MRS. FISHER (*after a pause*)

I'll bet there was five hundred dollars right on her back there to-day if there was a penny. And that's not counting her hat nor her shoes, either. (*There is another little pause*) That wig business must be a very good business. (*Aubrey looks over at her stonily; but she's occupied with her knitting*) I saw a piece in the *North American* the other morning, that a lot of people were wearing wigs now that don't need them at all. (*She looks over at Amy, to find Aubrey glaring at her*) That's what it said. (*He snaps his head round and continues reading*) She was telling me, Amy, that she lives in an apartment there in Chicago. Sez they couldn't *get* a house when they first went there. Sez there hasn't been a house go up in Chicago since before the war. (*She laughs faintly to herself*) I was telling her about the time you and Aubrey had, when you were first married — (*he looks over at her, with a dangerous squint*) trying to get even a couple of rooms somewhere. And the kind they were, when you *did* get them. (*She laughs a little more, at the recollection of them*) But they had the nerve to charge you nine dollars a month for them, just the same.

[*She smiles and looks at Aubrey.*

AUBREY (*explosively*)

I suppose you told her *that,* too, didn't you!

[*Amy is startled out of her interest in the newspaper.*

MRS. FISHER (*after a second's amazement*)

Told her what?

AUBREY

When were you handing out all this information?

AMY

Now, Aubrey, don't start, please!

AUBREY (*jumping to his feet*)

It's enough to *make* (*he slams the piece of newspaper down on to the chair violently*) a fellow start! (*He thrusts his hands into his trousers' pockets and strides towards the back of the room*) Trying to make me look like a poor *sap!*

[*He crosses to the hall door and right back again.*

MRS. FISHER (*looking in bewilderment at Amy*)

Why, what's the matter with *him!*

AMY and AUBREY (*together*)

⎰ (*Amy*) Nothing at all, Mother.
⎱ (*Aubrey, at the upper right-hand corner of the center table*)
You know very *well* what's the matter with me!

MRS. FISHER

What?

AUBREY

Handing out a line of *gab* about my *business!* every time you can get anybody to *listen* to you.

MRS. FISHER

Who was handing out any line of gab about your business?

AUBREY

You were! — and you're always doing it!

MRS. FISHER

Why, you haven't got any line of business for anybody to hand out any line of gab about — that I ever heard of.

[*She turns away.*

AUBREY

It doesn't matter whether I have any line of business or

not! It isn't necessary for you to be gabbing to perfect strangers about it.

MRS. FISHER

What did you want me to do, sit there lookin' at the woman, like a cow?

AMY

Mother, please.

AUBREY

You don't have to talk about my affairs!

MRS. FISHER (*with vast amusement*)

Your affairs —

AUBREY.

That's what I said, my affairs! (*Mrs. Fisher laughs derisively, and Aubrey turns to his wife, desperately*) You hear her!

MRS. FISHER

That's funny.

AMY

She wasn't talking about you, Aubrey.

AUBREY

She *was* talking about me! That's all she ever *does*, is talk about me!

[*Mrs. Fisher whirls around.*

MRS. FISHER

I was talkin' about houses! — that ain't you, is it?

AUBREY

I know what you were talking about, you needn't tell me.

MRS. FISHER

I had to talk about something, didn't I?

AMY

Keep quiet, Aubrey!

AUBREY and MRS. FISHER (*together*)

> (*Aubrey, whirling around and going towards the hall door*)
> No, I won't keep quiet!
> (*Mrs. Fisher*)   You two were down in the cellar fixing

the fire!   And you can't sit there with your two hands as long as each other when a person's visiting in your house!

AUBREY (*stopping abruptly above the center table, on his way back towards the portières*)

I suppose you mentioned *that*, too, didn't you!

MRS. FISHER (*half-turning and listening narrowly*)

Mentioned what?

AUBREY

That it was *your* house!

[*Mrs. Fisher turns her whole body round to him in a literal bounce.*

MRS. FISHER (*shrilly*)

Well, whose house *would* I mention that it was!

AUBREY (*turning to Amy with a broad gesture of his right hand*)

You see!   Didn't I tell you!

AMY and AUBREY (*together*)

> (*Amy*)   Well, what of it, Aubrey!   What of it!
> (*Aubrey*)   Every opportunity she gets she's trying to
> make me look like a poor thing!

[*He brings his right hand down thunderously upon the center table.   Then, thrusting his hands into his trousers' pockets again, strides over to the arched door and back again to the portières.*

MRS. FISHER (*after a strained pause*)

Why, what's the matter with the crazy Jack!

AMY

Pay no attention to him, Mother.

MRS. FISHER

I suppose I won't be able to say this house *is* my own after a while.

AUBREY (*stopping above the center table and rapping his fist upon it*)

It isn't necessary for you to be gabbing to perfect strangers about *whose* house it is!

MRS. FISHER (*keenly*)

I guess it'd have been all right if I'd told her it was yours, wouldn't it?

AUBREY (*repudiating her remark with a sharp gesture of his left hand*)

You don't have to tell anybody *anything*!

[*Mrs. Fisher springs to her feet.*

MRS. FISHER

I suppose that's what's the matter with you, isn't it?

AUBREY and MRS. FISHER (*together*)

{ (*Aubrey*) There's nothing at all the matter with me!
  [*He touches his handkerchief to his forehead.*
  (*Mrs. Fisher, taking a few steps towards Amy*) He's very likely been telling this friend of yours, Amy, that this is *his* house! And I guess with a lot of big talk about taking *me* in, and giving *me* a home! Trying to make *me* look like a poor thing!

AMY (*trying to pacify her mother*)

Now, he didn't tell her anything of the kind, Mother!

MRS. FISHER (*shaking with wrath*)

He did if he got the chance! I know him.

AMY

Well, he didn't *get* the chance; I was only out of the room two minutes.

MRS. FISHER (*returning to the sofa*)

Well, that's long enough for him! I've heard *him* before. (*She gathers up her knitting, preparatory to sitting
down*) Blowing his bubbles! (*She sits down, fuming*)
The big blatherskite! (*There is a pause. Amy and
Aubrey look at each other, then at Mrs. Fisher, who knits
violently*) I'm very glad now I *did* tell her this was my
house! — (*She knits a little more*) I'm glad I had
sense enough! (*More knitting*) For I know he'd very
soon tell her it was *his*, if he got my back turned long
enough! (*She draws some yarn from the ball*) And it
wouldn't be mine long, either, if I listened to all his silly
blather about stocks, and bonds, and automobiles, and
every other thing! — On his thirty-two dollars a week.
(*Aubrey looks stonily at her for a second; then she turns
sharply and leans on the arm of the sofa towards him*) I
told her *that*, too!

AUBREY (*turning to Amy, who is standing back of the armchair*)

You see! Didn't I tell you!

[*He passes forward at the right of his wife.*

MRS. FISHER (*resuming her knitting*)

So she'd know how much brains you had!

AMY

It wasn't at all necessary, Mother, for you to tell Marion
that.

MRS. FISHER (*without looking up from her work*)

Well, I told her; whether it was necessary or not.
(*She looks at Amy and speaks emphatically*) It was the
truth, anyway. And I guess that's more than can be
said for a whole lot that *he* told her.

[*She indicates Aubrey with a nod; then resumes her work.
There is a pause. Aubrey is standing fuming down at the*

right. Amy picks up the piece of the paper that he threw on the chair, then extends the piece that she has been reading towards him.

AMY

Do you want this?

AUBREY (*half-turning, and with a shade of hauteur*)

What is it?

AMY

Why, it's the newspaper of course! what do you think it is?

[*He deigns to take it. She gives him a long look, then opens the other half of the paper and reads.*

AUBREY (*opening his part of the paper*)

A man'd certainly have a swell chance trying to make anything of himself around this *hut!*

MRS. FISHER

I don't see that anybody's trying to *stop* you from making something of yourself.

AUBREY

No, and I don't see that anybody's trying to *help* me any, either. Only trying to make me look like a *pin-head* every chance they get.

MRS. FISHER

Nobody'll have to try very hard to make *you* look like a pin-head. Your own silly talk'll do *that* for you, any time at all.

AUBREY (*turning to her sharply*)

I suppose it's silly talk to try to make a good impression.

MRS. FISHER (*looking over at him, and inclining her head conclusively*)

Yes — It's silly to try to make an impression of *any*

kind; for the only one that'll be made'll be the *right* one; and that'll make itself.

[*She reverts to her work.*

AUBREY

Well, if you were out in the world as much as I am, you'd very soon see how much easier it is for a fellow to get along if people think he's *got* something.

MRS. FISHER

Well, anybody listen to you very long'd know you *couldn't* have very much.

AUBREY

Is that so.

MRS. FISHER (*quietly*)

You heard me. (*Aubrey steps over to the armchair at his left and sits down, looking bitterly at his mother-in-law*) People that are smart enough to be able to make it easier for anybody, are not interested in what you've got. (*Looking over at him*) It's what you've got in your *brains* that they're interested in.   And nobody has to tell them that, either.   They'll know all about it, if you never opened your mouth.

AMY

Oh, stop talking, Mother.

[*She turns, with a movement of wearied impatience, from the right end of the center table, and crosses over back of the armchair to the right, where she continues to read. There is a quiet pause; Amy and Aubrey reading, and Mrs. Fisher knitting. Then Aubrey looks up from his paper, thinks for a second, and half turns to his wife.*

AUBREY

Did you get that remark your friend made, as she was going out?

AMY

What remark?

[*Mrs. Fisher looks over.*

AUBREY (*with a self-satisfied smile*)

About the best-looking man in Philadelphia?

MRS. FISHER (*rearranging her knitting*)

Oh, dear!

[*Aubrey gives her a narrow look; then turns back to his wife.*

AUBREY

She made it twice, too.

AMY

I suppose I'll never hear the end of that now.

AUBREY

No, but it made an awful hit with me, after all the talk you made about putting on the toupee.

AMY

Oh, it wasn't the toupee that made her say it; don't flatter yourself.

AUBREY

I don't think it hurt any.

AMY

No, and I don't think you're so crazy about the toupee yourself.

AUBREY

It's better than being baldheaded.

AMY

I notice you got rid of it very quickly, as soon as she went.

[*Mrs. Fisher listens.*

AUBREY

What?

AMY (*without looking up from the paper*)

You heard me. (*Mrs. Fisher can't resist a glance at Aubrey; but realizing that her expression might precipitate another row, she turns away quietly and continues with her knitting. Aubrey hasn't grasped the significance of his wife's remark. He turns and looks at her with a puzzled expression; but she is reading; so he turns back again and looks straight out, baffled. Then a thought occurs to him. He reaches up and touches his head. The toupee is off. His brows lift and his mouth falls open, and he sits staring straight ahead for a second. Then he glances furtively at his mother-in-law, but she is studiously avoiding the situation. He gets up, very quietly; and, with a little glance over his right shoulder at his wife, turns and gives a quick look on the armchair and under it. No sign of the toupee. He feels all over his head and around the back of his neck; puts his hand up under his coat, and looks on the floor back of the armchair. All very quietly, and with a pathetic attempt at nonchalance. But the toupee is not to be seen. He saunters up towards the back of the room, steps over and glances at himself in the mirror, then stands looking about the floor in a quandary. His wife observes him out of the corner of her eye, and turns to him*) What are you looking for?

[*He glances at Mrs. Fisher, then goes very close to his wife and speaks in a confidential tone.*

AUBREY

My toupee. Did you see anything of it?

AMY

Where'd you put it?

AUBREY (*with a shade of impatience*)

I didn't put it anywhere.

AMY

Well, where did you have it?

AUBREY (*becoming more impatient*)

I had it on my head, of course! where'd you think I had it!

AMY

I thought you took it off, when Marion went.

AUBREY

No, I didn't take it off!

AMY

Well, where is it?

AUBREY (*throwing discretion to the winds*)

I don't know *where* it is! That's why I'm asking *you!* (*Mrs. Fisher can no longer contain herself, and bursts into unrestrained laughter. They both turn sharply and look at her, Aubrey glaring*) Funny! isn't it!
[*Amy crosses quickly to the center table, in front of her husband.*

AMY

Did you see anything of it, Mother?

MRS. FISHER (*bursting out afresh*)

I saw it *fall off*, that's all *I* know about it.
[*They stand looking at her.*

AUBREY

You see that! She'd let me walk around here all day with it off, and never tip me off that it was off!

MRS. FISHER

What good was it to tip you off that it was off after it was off! (*Turning back to her knitting*) The cat was out of the bag, then.

AMY

Where'd it fall off, Mother?

MRS. FISHER

When he was picking that woman's glove up, up there at the hallway. (*Amy turns quickly towards the hall door, glancing about the floor; and Mrs. Fisher turns to Aubrey*) It isn't *my* fault if his old *wig* doesn't fit him.

[*He is looking at her with murder in his eye; but she does'nt flinch. If anything, there is a glint of challenge in her look. And it's quite as steady as his own. Amy finds the toupee where it fell, and holds it up towards Aubrey by one hair.*

AMY

Is this it?

[*But the duel of eyes is still on between Aubrey and his mother-in-law; and he is oblivious of both his wife and her question. So the toupee, looking very much like a dead cat, depends from Amy's uplifted fingers. Then, suddenly, Aubrey snatches it, with a whirling movement to the left, and goes towards the mirror to adjust it.*

MRS. FISHER (*following him with her eyes*)

It just serves him right! That's what he gets for showing off!

AUBREY (*whirling at the mirror, and literally shouting at her*)

Shut up, will you!

[*The violence of his turning sends the toupee flying off his head on to the floor, and causes Mrs. Fisher to start so that her ball of yarn flies four feet into the air.*

AMY (*taking a step towards her husband and lifting her hand to enjoin silence*)

Sh — sh — sh —

AUBREY (*looking at her with an eye of fire*)

I won't stand much more of this Amy! now, I'm telling you!

AMY

Keep quiet, Aubrey! Marion probably never noticed it at all.

MRS. FISHER

I don't know how she could *help* noticing it. *I* noticed it; and I don't think my eyesight's as good as hers.

AUBREY

Then, why didn't you say something!

MRS. FISHER

Because I knew if I did I'd very likely get snatched baldheaded!

[*Aubrey starts violently, and Mrs. Fisher snaps back to her knitting.*

AUBREY (*appealing to his wife*)

You hear that! Is it any wonder my nerves are the way they are!

AMY

Oh, keep quiet, Aubrey! for Heaven's sake! (*Pointing to the toupee on the floor, as she steps forward at the right of the center table*) And pick up your wig.

[*This is too much for Aubrey. He literally sways against the portières above the mirror.*

AUBREY (*recovering himself*)

It isn't a wig, now, Amy! I've told you that a half a dozen times!

AMY (*looking up from the paper which she has commenced to read, and in an exhausted tone*)

Well, then, pick up your toupee!

[*He picks it up and simply slaps it back on to his head. The effect is weird; for it is quite disheveled from its recent experiences, and, in his temper, he has put it on backwards. He swings forward at the right and sits in the armchair, very sulkily.   Amy crosses over back of the armchair and stands down near the little table at the right, where she continues to read the evening paper.   Mrs. Fisher knits, and Aubrey sits sulking, looking straight ahead.   There is a pause.   Then, possibly at the recollection of certain of the remarks that his mother-in-law made earlier in the battle, Aubrey darts a sudden glare in her direction; only to find that she has been the victim of similar memories.   So they sit and scowl at each other; then turn away.   Then turn back again, and away again.   Then Aubrey becomes conscious of his wife; and of the fact that she is reading the evening newspaper; and, by the association of ideas, his thought is diverted into more becoming channels.   He half-turns to Amy, with something of the self-importance that characterized his earlier manner, and, after a slight pause, addresses her.*

AUBREY

Have you got the — a — financial page there?

[Amy hands it to him; and the curtain commences to descend very slowly.

MRS. FISHER

Hum!

[He glares over at her, but she's knitting; so, withdrawing his eyes, he reaches into his vest pocket and brings forth the rimmed nose-glasses, which he settles rather authentically upon his nose.   Then he takes a silver pencil from the other vest pocket, and, turning to his wife, accepts the newspaper.   Then he crosses his knees, and, spreading the newspaper upon them, proceeds to figure profits in the margin.   Amy stands looking at him, and Mrs. Fisher knits.

THE CURTAIN IS DOWN